REPATTERNED

How to Transform Your Conflict Defaults
and Reclaim Your Life

MASHA RUSANOV

Cover design by Judith S. Design & Creativity

www.judithsdesign.com

Published by Glass Spider Publishing

www.glassspiderpublishing.com

For the whole, wild, blended constellation of people
I call family.

You taught me how complicated love can be and
how much beauty lives inside the mess.

This book is stitched together from everything we lived.

Contents

Acknowledgments...7

Introduction 9

Chapter 1: How We Learn About Conflict 16

Chapter 2: Impulse – When the Body Speaks First 28

Chapter 3: Habit – The Pattern That Follows 41

Chapter 4: The Exhale–Explore–Engage Method 56

Chapter 5: Exhale – Feel the Shift 66

Chapter 6: Explore – Find the Pattern 80

Chapter 7: Engage – Flip the Script..93

Chapter 8: When the Conflict Is Within You 112

Chapter 9: When It's Family..130

Chapter 10: Conflict with Your Partner...................................146

Chapter 11: Conflict with Friends and Community 161

Chapter 12: Conflict at Work 177

Chapter 13: Dealing With High-Conflict Personalities..............191

Chapter 14: When to Walk Away................................209

Chapter 15: Living the Exhale–Explore–Engage Method..........223

Bonus Materials 234

Crisis & Safety Resources 243

References 245

About the Author.......................................248

Acknowledgments

I didn't write this book alone. I wrote it in the middle of life: between school drop-offs, coaching sessions, classes, conflict, and healing. Every chapter carries the fingerprints of the people who sat with me, challenged me, held me accountable, or simply didn't give up on me when I retreated into old patterns.

To my family—the large, layered, always-evolving group of people that made me who I am. You are my teachers in conflict, connection, acceptance, love, and resilience.

To my husband, Anton, for loving me through every draft, every doubt, and every moment when I reverted to an old pattern. Thank you for your steadiness, your presence, and your willingness to grow alongside me.

To Fedor—the rare ex-husband who co-parents with grace, humor, and genuine friendship. Thank you for modeling that a committed post-marriage partnership is possible, and for choosing peace, even when it left me almost no material to practice conflict resolution on!

To Charlie and Olga—two people who never intended to become teachers in my life, yet offered me some of the most transformative growth I've ever had.

To my friend Thea—you held my hand through this entire process. Thank you for organizing my chaos, grounding me when I drifted, and reminding me what I'm trying to say when I forgot. This book would not exist without your steady presence.

To Martha Beck—whose brilliant work on integrity, body wisdom, and wayfinding showed me a way to stop abandoning myself and gave me the courage to focus on what truly mattered.

To my professor, Lucia Galante Johnson—you opened doors in my mind I didn't know existed. Your classes reshaped the way I see conflict, power, and possibility. I have carried your wisdom into every chapter.

To my clients—thank you for trusting me with your hardest stories, your conflicts, your hopes, and your heartbreaks. You taught me how universal these patterns are, and how brave people can be when they choose to show up differently.

And finally, to the version of myself who kept showing up. The one who chose breath over panic, truth over performance, and presence over legacy patterns. You wrote this. One word, one idea, one exhale at a time.

Introduction

For most of us, conflict ranks alongside doing taxes or assembling flat-pack furniture: something to dread, avoid, or simply survive with minimal emotional (or actual) disassembly. Whether it's an argument with a partner, tension at work, or a loud inner critic, conflict can feel overwhelming, messy, and painful. We may worry that we will do damage to others or to the relationships we care about. Yet rather than approach the situation with care, too often our old patterns take over in ways that do not help in the moment. We shut down, lash out, or try to frantically smooth things over—all in an attempt to keep the peace.

But what if conflict could be something more?

What if every disagreement were an opportunity to grow, to reconnect with what matters, and to strengthen, rather than damage, relationships?

That might sound impossible. I thought so, too. For a long time, I thought conflict was something to be avoided whenever possible, or, if unavoidable, then simply endured. I never considered that it could offer something that could shape me into a stronger, wiser, and more grounded version of myself. And yet I know now there is a path to becoming repatterned from the inside out—a way to get off autopilot and intentionally choose a different path.

Let me tell you my story.

The café was too bright. Fluorescent lights hummed overhead, and someone's laptop played tinny music from three tables away. My first husband, Fedor, sat across from me, stirring his coffee with a spoon though he'd added nothing to it. Round and round. The sound was like a metronome counting down to something neither of us wanted to say.

Our marriage wasn't working.

We both knew it.

Knowing it and saying it were different animals entirely.

My heart was doing that thing it does, beating too fast and too slow at the same time. My hands felt cold. I was acutely aware of the distance between our chairs, maybe three feet that felt like a canyon. I noticed his jaw muscle tightening. He was about to say something important, and my whole body braced for impact.

The thought arrived before I could stop it: This is the end. Right here in this café with the bad lighting and the stranger's laptop music. This is where we fall apart.

And then came my familiar exit strategy. My mind started calculating. If I leave now, I can be at my car in two minutes. I can drive somewhere quiet. I can avoid whatever words are coming because words can't be taken back, and this feels like the kind of conversation that leaves scars.

I could feel myself retreating, pulling inward like a turtle into its shell. My vision actually narrowed. Fedor was still stirring his coffee, but I was already gone, just a body in a chair while the real me hovered somewhere near the ceiling, preparing for emergency evacuation.

My chest was so tight I thought I might be having a heart attack. The room felt smaller. I wanted to disappear into the floor tiles. Every cell in my body was screaming: *Get out. Get out before he says it. Get out before you have to respond. Get out before this becomes real.*

And then, something shifted.

It wasn't dramatic. Just a tiny crack in the pattern, barely perceptible. A thought, quiet beneath all the panic: *What if I stayed?*

Not stayed in the marriage. Just stayed in this moment. *What if I didn't run? What if I didn't shut down? What if I took one breath and let him speak, and then took another breath before I responded?*

The idea felt radical. Terrifying, even. Staying meant feeling. Feeling meant pain. But leaving, I realized, meant something worse. Leaving meant I'd never know what could have happened if I'd been brave enough to remain present for the hard part.

So I took one breath. Deliberately. I felt my feet on the floor, the solidness of the chair beneath me. I unclenched my hands. And I looked at Fedor, really looked at him, for the first time in months. His eyes were tired. His shoulders were hunched. He was afraid, too.

That breath didn't save our marriage. We divorced anyway. But that breath, that single moment of choosing presence over panic, changed everything that came after.

Instead of following my first reaction (to shut down) or my urge to flee, I chose to pause, to listen, and to view my husband and myself with new eyes. In that moment, choosing differently meant *thinking* instead of reacting from fear. I was able to engage and share something from a different place without a heavy load of emotions, and my husband was able to hear where I was coming from without feeling pressured or attacked. My vulnerability allowed us to explore possibilities we hadn't considered, ultimately leading us to navigate what had felt like irreconcilable differences in a way that prioritized mutual respect, growth, and compassion. Choosing a different way to respond during an emotionally tense time enabled us to have an amazing co-parenting relationship and post-divorce friendship. We now celebrate holidays and birthdays together with our kids and our new spouses; we travel together and call each other regularly for support and advice.

We all have to deal with conflicts. Maybe for you, the moment of inescapable conflict didn't happen in a café but in an air-conditioned office. Imagine you're in a performance review, and your boss slides a list of areas where you need improvement across the table. The review feels like a personal attack. Your heart hammers against your ribs, and a hot flush of shame or anger creeps up your neck. The old pattern screams at you to defend yourself—to list all the reasons why your boss is wrong—or to simply shut down, nod, and retreat to your desk to replay the conversation in your head, on repeat.

But what if, in that moment, you could take a single, silent breath? What if you could notice the defensiveness rising and instead of letting it speak for you, you could choose to ask a question from a place of genuine curiosity: "Can you help me understand that better with a specific example?" In that simple shift is the moment you stop being a victim of the conversation—and start shaping it.

Conflict isn't always with another person—sometimes the conflict is internal—between you and the loud, critical voice in your head. You're staring at a spreadsheet in a job that pays the bills but drains your soul, dreaming of a different career. But your inner critic is relentless in shutting down your hopes for the future: *You're too old to start over. You're not talented enough. You'll fail, and everyone will see.* The familiar response is to surrender—to push the dream down, close the laptop, and accept the quiet misery of the "safe" path. But pausing here looks like acknowledging that voice of fear without needing to obey it. It's choosing to take one tiny, manageable step—researching a class, sending a single email, or sketching out a business idea on a napkin—as a quiet declaration that your future is still up for discussion.

Conflict does not have to be a battlefield. Even when the tensions run high, there is still a way to get to a resolution with grace. It doesn't always have to end in victory or defeat. Sometimes it ends in a deeper kind of honesty. Sometimes it ends in freedom.

And if I was able to change the script, so can you. The moment we realize we don't have to be stuck with our first response, we unlock something that's been waiting to breathe. When we meet hard moments with a pause, we open up a space for clarity instead of panic and reclaim our power, even when the outcome is not what we hoped for.

I want to show you how.

I will teach you how to become someone who does not get overwhelmed by emotions in the heat of the moment, but rather someone who knows how to stay present even when the heat rises—

someone who can feel the body bracing, the mind racing, and who can still *choose* to respond rather than react, even if that means walking away.

My method is a simple yet powerful framework I built for people who want to stay grounded and conscious in any situation. It is designed to help you notice when your emotions are trying to hijack the steering wheel and to be able to use the tools I give you to pull over, breathe, and choose what happens next.

Before we begin, it is essential to be clear about what this framework is for—and what it is *not* for. Your safety is ALWAYS the priority. This method is designed for addressing internal conflict and navigating challenging conversations and disagreements in relationships. It is *not* a tool for situations involving abuse, harassment, or physical or psychological danger. If you are in a situation where you feel unsafe, the goal is to get to safety and seek help from appropriate sources, such as a domestic violence hotline, law enforcement, or your company's HR department. I included a list in the Bonus Materials section.

Now, let me tell you what my method is. It consists of three simple steps, but don't let the simplicity fool you. Each one is powerful.

Exhale grounds you in your body.

Explore invites you to be curious rather than spiral into judgment.

Engage brings you back into the moment, allowing you to speak or act from a place that feels genuine, from your truth.

The more you practice it, the more it becomes muscle memory. It's like learning to ride a bike, except the handlebars are emotional regulation, and the brakes are self-awareness and conscious choice.

You don't have to read this book straight through. It's a companion. Pick a chapter that fits the fight you're facing now—internal battles, work drama, family or relationship chaos—and let it meet you where you are.

You'll find prompts, body-based practices, and tools that work, even when everything in you wants to bolt. And when you need support, you can dive into the online guided resources at www.repatternedbook.com. They're there for the messy days, the brave days, and everything in between.

Your clarity is already inside you. Although you may not realize it, your voice is there too, just beneath the noise. This book won't give you something you don't already have. It will help you remember what's always been yours.

One breath.

One pause.

One conscious choice at a time.

Chapter 1: How We Learn About Conflict

"We repeat what we don't repair." –Christine Langley-Obaugh

When I was little, I learned that the safest thing I could do in a moment of conflict was to disappear. At my daycare, whenever a child got too loud or broke a rule, the teachers didn't just scold; they screamed. Sometimes they punished those kids by shaming them in front of everyone or making them stand in the corner in their underwear for hours at a time. Mind you, that was in snowy Siberia, and even though we had heating systems, the temperature wasn't always ideal for that sort of thing. I was stressed out and terrified, and I was too young to understand and process what was happening. However, I adapted. Whenever someone broke the rules and the "disciplining" took place, I pretended to be asleep or hid somewhere. I froze. I made myself small, trained myself (quite successfully!) to be so quiet, obedient, and still, that I wouldn't be noticed. My nervous system learned that when I didn't speak up and instead obeyed, I would be left alone. I learned that *silence equals safety.*

Dealing with stressful situations during childhood is how our nervous systems begin to learn what conflict means and how to deal with it through the body. As kids, we know instinctively when to hide, when to run, when to do whatever it is that will help us feel safe.

We carry those lessons forward, often without even realizing it.

Later, in fifth grade, the lesson deepened.

My best friend, Kate, stopped speaking to me on a Tuesday. No warning. No fight. One day, we were sharing secrets at lunch, and the next, she walked past me like I was furniture. When I tried to catch her eye, she looked through me. When I asked what happened, she turned away.

The rest of our friend group followed within days. Six girls who had been my whole social world suddenly became a wall of silence. I'd approach the lunch table, and they'd go quiet. I'd enter the classroom, and they'd drift to the other side. I spent recess walking the perimeter of the schoolyard alone, trying to look like that was the most exciting activity one could imagine for their break.

I became obsessed with fixing it. I wrote Kate a note asking what I'd done wrong. No response. I tried being extra nice to everyone, complimenting their hair, sharing my snacks. They took the snacks but kept their distance. I analyzed every interaction from the weeks before, searching for the moment I'd made the fatal mistake. Had I laughed too loudly? Said something wrong? Worn the wrong thing?

The silence lasted three weeks. In fifth-grade time, that's an eternity.

It wasn't until a teacher noticed me eating lunch alone in the hallway that anything changed. She intervened, called the girls together, mediated some kind of conversation I wasn't part of. The next day, Katya said hi to me in the morning. Just like that, I was allowed back.

But I was different. Something had calcified inside me. I spent the rest of that school year being very, very careful. I laughed at the right jokes. I agreed with the group opinion. I made myself smaller, lighter, easier. I learned that belonging was conditional and could be revoked without explanation. The lessons that solidified for the young me were clear.

Conflict means you are not safe.

Conflict means you are excluded.

Conflict means you are alone.

And underneath all of that: If people leave, it's probably your fault. Figure out what you did wrong, and fix it before they notice.

⌒Ask yourself: What did conflict look like in your home, daycare, or early friendships? Was it loud? Silent? Passive-aggressive? Explosive?

What Happens to Our Body During Conflict

Today, we talk a lot about communication styles and tools for challenging conversations. There is no shortage of advice on how to speak up, set boundaries, or validate someone else's experience. Those tools are incredibly useful when you remember to use them. When conflict hits, though, most of us aren't calmly pulling out our best communication technique. We're reacting. Fast. Often unconsciously. Because we're flooded, and something deep in our nervous system has already decided we're in danger and turned that moment into a survival event.

Our nervous system is wired to react quickly, to keep us safe, rather than give us a chance to calmly figure out the best communication tool to use during those emotionally charged moments. This is not a flaw in our character, nor is it immaturity or oversensitivity. It's biology.

Have you ever reacted to someone with a flash of defensiveness, only to realize moments later that your response was completely out of proportion? You ended up apologizing, but the mystery remains: Why did you react that way?

This gap between the triggering event and our oversized reaction is where our biology lives. It's the result of a silent, lightning-fast verdict being delivered by our body. A groundbreaking theory in psychology finally gives us the language to understand exactly how that verdict is reached before we even have a chance to think.

Through his *polyvagal theory*, psychologist Stephen Porges introduced the concept of *neuroception*, the body's ability to detect safety or danger cues without our conscious attention. Neuroception is our body's highly sensitive, yet slightly paranoid, internal security system that constantly scans the environment for potential threats. Neuroception explains why someone's sigh, slightly tense expression, or a particular kind of silence can trigger an inner alarm before our thinking brain gets involved. What we sense through tone, posture, or facial expression leads to a swift, automatic question: *Am I safe here?*

In those moments, we don't choose our reactions—our bodies do. We don't decide to go numb, to shut down, or to lash out. Our body makes that choice based on an entire history of unresolved tensions and emotional ruptures that happened to us during our lifetimes. Trauma therapist Deb Dana calls this your *autonomic story*, a narrative your body tells through sensation and reaction rather than words. It's the emotional script your nervous system wrote long before you could explain it.

Once that story is triggered, the *amygdala*, the brain's emotional alarm center, takes over. Our amygdalae, bless their well-intentioned hearts, aren't exactly known for their nuanced interpretation of social cues during heated discussions. They have a "sound the alarm and ask questions later" response.

Daniel Goleman popularized the phrase *amygdala hijack* to describe what happens in these moments. The brain releases cortisol and adrenaline, causing the prefrontal cortex, the area of the brain responsible for reasoning and regulation, to go offline. Suddenly, our brain's sophisticated language processing center turns off, replaced by a far more primitive amygdala-driven script. Then, you might ask, what happens to curiosity and compassion? They've left the building, likely calling for a backup that won't arrive until the perceived threat has departed.

During an amygdala hijack, our breath shortens, and our thoughts speed up or shut down. Our tone of voice changes, and we might stop responding in the present moment and slip into old, unconscious patterns of reacting. Conflict then becomes less about what is happening in the here and now and more about the echoes of everything we have experienced before that felt even remotely similar and remains unresolved.

⟲Ask yourself: What's your go-to reaction in conflict? Do you shut down? Get loud? Numb out? What do you think your body is trying to protect you from in those moments?

You are Not Broken—You are Patterned

For a long time, I thought something was wrong with me. Why did I freeze in conversations that mattered most? Why couldn't I speak up until it was too late or until I exploded? Why did I leave arguments feeling shaky and ashamed?

I saw these reactions as personal failings. I thought I needed to learn how to get over shutting down by learning more self-help tools and being more rational and less emotional. I read over 300 self-help books; they even wrote an article about me in *Newsweek*! What I *actually* needed was to understand my patterns.

When conflict arises and we react, most of us subconsciously draw on a protective system that was built years or even decades ago. Maybe it started when your parents yelled, and you went silent to avoid punishment. Or when you spoke up and got laughed at, ignored, or shut down. We may be reluctant to speak up again, remembering the consequences that followed. Those moments don't just pass through us; they *shape us*. They leave a neurological and emotional imprint that forms a pattern. Unless we've had the tools, time, and support to process and repattern those responses, we carry them into every interaction.

Most of us don't reflect on our conflict responses; we just live them. We inherit, absorb, and rehearse them until they feel like part of our personality. But they are not who we truly are. In fact, looking closely at them often stirs shame, because these are moments when we don't show up as our most mature selves. Instead, we act in ways driven by unconscious parts of us.

Internal Family Systems (IFS) and some other behavioral analysis models characterize these as ego states or parts as ways of thinking, feeling, and behaving that make up a person's personality at any given time. They should not be considered as flaws; they are adaptations, patterns that we had to adopt to feel safe. Alongside the reactive parts (called "firefighters"), we also have proactive *manager parts*, inner organizers who work tirelessly to prevent future pain by managing, planning, perfecting, or avoiding risk. Beneath both of them are the *exiled parts*—tender, often very young inner parts that carry the pain and beliefs we've had to bury in order to function.

Most of our reactive behaviors didn't begin as choices; they started as protective mechanisms. You can't shame yourself out of a pattern that was designed to keep you safe. Even the sharpest self-awareness won't change a thing if it's not met with compassion. I eventually realized I couldn't just think my way out of my patterns; they were too deep, too wired in to change them through sheer intention. To really understand them, I had to go back to where they started—not to dwell on the past but to gently see the blueprint it had left on me. It was only by tracing these lines that I could start to see where I had the power to draw new ones.

This was one of the first and most powerful exercises I did for myself, and it opened the door to so much understanding. I invite you to try it, just as I did.

Exercise: Trace Your Conflict Blueprint

Reflect on how conflict felt in your early life. This exercise will help you begin identifying the emotional blueprints that shape your reactions today. Here is how you can explore this:

1. Close your eyes and recall a childhood memory involving conflict. Don't analyze, just let a scene come to mind.

2. Ask:
   o What happened at that moment?
   o How did your body respond?
   o What belief did you take away from that experience? What did you decide?

3. Complete these sentences:
   o "In conflict, I learned that I had to _________ in order to be okay."
   o "I decided that I will never/always _________ from now on."

4. Reflect:
   o What role did you adopt? Appeaser? The one who hides? Attacker? Peacemaker? Finger-pointer? Defender? Something else?
   o How does the role you learned then (e.g., appeaser, hider, attacker) get praised or rewarded in your adult life now? Did you experience the relief of avoiding a potential argument? Or maybe it allowed you to stay under the radar and not get yelled at.

Once you begin to see your patterns for what they are—survival strategies—you might notice things shifting. However, it is important to remember that even with all that awareness, some moments of conflict will still hit like a wave because recognizing your pattern does not mean your nervous system has caught up. Beneath the surface of every reaction lies something deeper: the meaning we attach to what is happening, our beliefs and assumptions, our stories, and the interpretations we make—*the invisible conclusions we jump to before a single word has landed.*

The Story Beneath the Words

You can be sitting across from someone you love, having what seems like a reasonable disagreement, and still feel like you are unraveling inside. Their *no* is heard as *I don't respect you.* An unanswered text becomes the feeling that *I don't matter.* Your body translates their audible sigh as they walk away into one painful conclusion: *I messed everything up.*

Often, what hurts most is not the words themselves, but *what we believe* they mean. Some part of you knows it's not a big deal, but another part reacts as if it's a complete disaster. That's the invisible layer of conflict—the meaning we attach to it.

That leap, from behavior to belief, happens in a flash because we rarely slow down enough to question it, and the story becomes our reality. Just last week, a friend texted *Can we talk later?*

My mind immediately spiraled. *What did I do? She's mad at me! She's ending the friendship!!!* I felt a familiar dread settle in my stomach. When we finally spoke, she just wanted to ask for a book recommendation. My brain had written an entire tragedy based on four neutral words.

I remember when a coworker yelled at me for a mistake I made. He was a large man who towered over me, his face red, his fists clenched, scolding me for something he thought I hadn't handled well during a customer meeting. I don't remember what exactly he was saying I did wrong, but what hit me was the volume and the intensity of his voice. I froze. I sat there slumped on the couch, completely still, while he finished his tirade. When he was done, I managed to say, "Okay," and quietly walk out of the room. I spent the next half hour crying in a bathroom stall.

It was not just embarrassment or guilt that was washing over me. It was something older and deeper than that. I didn't realize it then, but it was the pattern that my nervous system had reverted to from the daycare days of my childhood: the screaming teachers, the threat of punishment, and the sense that when you mess up, you deserve to be shamed. I was not just reacting to this man; I was reacting to the story *I'm bad. I'm not safe. I shouldn't be here.*

Another time, my son didn't answer when I asked him something. I spiraled immediately. I started questioning my parenting, wondering what I'd done wrong, feeling like a failure. In a split second, my mind has decided: *He's ignoring me → I must be a bad mom.*

Then I saw the headphones in his ears. He literally couldn't hear me. Before I noticed the headphones, my inner drama queen had already launched a one-woman show called *How I Met Your (Terrible) Mother.*

When conflict arises, our brains fill the gaps with old material. We go from a look, a pause, or a word—straight into a wound. We react not only to the moment but also to every experience it evokes. For example:

He raised his voice becomes *I'm not worthy.*

She didn't text back becomes *I don't matter.*

They disagreed with me becomes *They don't love me.*

They were quiet becomes *I did something wrong.*

That leap, from behavior to belief, happens in a flash because we rarely slow down enough to question it, and the story becomes our reality.

♡Ask yourself: What does your mind typically assume during conflict? Do your thoughts jump to "I must be wrong" or "They're going to leave" or "I'm not allowed to feel this way"?

These internal beliefs are often subconscious. They were shaped early in environments when we had little power, yet needed to stay safe emotionally, physically, and relationally. If you had to earn attention and love from a relative, were punished for expressing yourself, or were ignored until you were perfect, your nervous system remembers it all.

Even today, in conversations that seem low stakes to others, your body may still respond intensely, as if everything is on the line. That's not being dramatic. That's your nervous system protecting you in a way that used to keep you safe.

The stories you carry into conflict aren't truths; they are *interpretations*. Like any story, they can be questioned, softened, and rewritten. It's like wearing your childhood glasses into every adult interaction. Everything gets distorted so that silence looks like disapproval. Frustration feels like abandonment.

⏻Ask yourself: What kinds of lenses do you think you inherited or learned? What situations have felt distorted recently?

Thankfully, with some intention and practices that I'm about to share with you, you can take off these old glasses. With the right tools, you can begin to clean the lenses, adjust their focus, and, even if only for a moment, remove them. If you stay with it, eventually you will not need them at all. When you understand what your nervous system is doing in that moment, you can begin to pause, breathe, and make space for a new response.

What you've learned in this chapter:
o *Conflict reactions are wired through early experiences.*
o *Your nervous system creates a "conflict blueprint" based on childhood dynamics.*
o *Exploring your early conflict experiences can reveal deeply ingrained patterns.*
o *Pausing lets you notice the lens you're reacting through and question it.*

Chapter 2: Impulse – When the Body Speaks First

"Being able to feel safe with other people is probably the single most important aspect of mental health." –*Bessel van der Kolk*

Before you say a word, or even register what's happening in an emotionally charged situation, something shifts inside you. It's subtle but unmistakable. Your body reacts—you might notice some tightening, pulling back, speeding up, or shutting down. This is known as *impulse*. It is fast, automatic, and deeply wired. That impulse comes from the part of your nervous system designed to keep you safe. If you've ever thought *I don't know why I just did that* or wished you could rewind a conversation, what you experienced was impulse in action.

Take, for example, the story of my coworker raising his voice at me. I froze. My breath turned shallow, and my whole body went stiff. I didn't plan that reaction; it happened before I could think. That was an *impulse*. If my body hadn't taken over, I would have chosen a very different way to respond.

For many years, I judged myself harshly for the way I reacted to situations like that. I have since learned that what happens in those moments is not a failure of willpower but the nervous system reacting as it has been patterned to respond to a perceived threat. It's automatic.

⌒Ask yourself: Can you think of a time when you reacted quickly in conflict, maybe even surprised yourself? What did it feel like in your body? What did you do?

Impulse is your nervous system's best attempt to keep you safe, but it can only draw on what it already knows. If what it knows is fear, silence, pleasing, freezing, or defending, then that's what it will use until you begin giving it new experiences—new ways to respond, to draw from.

Once you understand what's happening in that first instant before the words, before the story, you can start to create space to consciously *respond* rather than react.

Your Inner Alarm System

Your impulse in conflict is not random. We've talked about how your nervous system constantly scans your environment for signs of threat, even before your brain catches up. This process of neuroception sets the stage for what happens next: If something feels off—a tone of voice, a glance, a shift in body language—your body does not wait for evidence; it reacts. It's your internal fire alarm, and it was conditioned to go off at the smell of burnt toast rather than wait to confirm whether there is an actual fire.

These processes take place in the *autonomic nervous system*, which keeps us alive by regulating functions outside of our conscious awareness. Our reactions tend to fall into one of four classic patterns: *fight, flight, freeze,* or *fawn.*

In the Internal Family Systems model, these lightning-fast reactions are often driven by the *firefighter parts.* These parts spring into action to stop overwhelming emotional distress, often through impulsive, dramatic efforts to extinguish the pain, no matter the collateral damage. They're called "firefighters" because they behave much like real firefighters do in dousing a blaze—they rapidly deploy whatever means necessary to quell immediate emotional threats, even if those methods will have significant consequences.

Fight, flight, freeze, and *fawn* are your nervous system's first line of defense when it senses a threat. Depending on the situation, you may lean heavily on one or shift between them. They aren't flaws. They're survival strategies, shaped by past experiences. Learning to recognize your dominant impulse is the first step toward creating space, awareness, and ultimately a choice in how you respond to conflict.

Fight does not always look like physical aggression. It can be defensiveness, arguing, sarcasm, or trying to dominate or manipulate the situation to regain control.

Flight may not mean physically leaving the room. It may entail changing the subject, mentally checking out, overworking, or pretending to be asleep.

Freeze is the body's automatic stilling response. You shut down, go numb, and don't know what to say, so you say nothing.

Fawn is the impulse to please, smooth things over, or say what the other person wants to hear so the conflict disappears.

In my case, my default in stressful situations was to freeze. It's the reaction I have practiced since childhood, when disappearing felt like the safest option. When teachers yelled or punished kids unpredictably at daycare, I learned that stillness was protection. That response became so ingrained that even decades later, my body continued to default to the same survival strategy in adult conflicts. I remember a disagreement with a friend that was becoming heated. Even though we were both adults, my body started doing what it always did: went quiet, still, immobile.

Freeze-to-fawn pattern is what I know best. But I've worked with enough people to know that survival shows up in many languages.

My client Marcus, a software engineer in his forties, had a completely different blueprint. His impulse was to fight. When he sensed tension, whether it was a disagreement with his wife about finances or a colleague questioning his code, his body went hot. His jaw would tighten, his voice would drop to a dangerous calm, and he'd start dismantling the other person's argument with surgical precision. He didn't yell. He destroyed.

"I call it my prosecutor mode," he told me in our first session. "I get so calm. So logical. And I absolutely eviscerate them."

Marcus's childhood had been chaotic. His father drank, and his mother would erupt unpredictably. As a kid, Marcus learned that the person who controlled the conversation controlled the outcome. If he could out-argue, out-logic, out-debate anyone in the room, he'd be safe. His intelligence became his weapon.

The problem was that his wife wasn't his opponent. His colleagues weren't adversaries. But his nervous system couldn't tell the difference. Every disagreement became a courtroom, and Marcus had to win or something terrible would happen. He wasn't sure what, exactly. Just that losing felt like dying.

Another client, Priya, was pure flight. When things got tense, she'd physically leave. She had a reputation at work for being "unreliable" because she'd disappear mid-project when stress peaked. She'd quit jobs right before performance reviews. She'd ended two engagements by literally moving to different cities without much explanation. "I just need space to think," she'd say. But what she was doing was running.

Priya grew up in a household where emotions were overwhelming. Her parents' fights were loud and long, filling every corner of the house. As a child, she'd escape to her room, put on headphones, and disappear into books. Leaving became her superpower. If she wasn't there, she couldn't be hurt.

As an adult, that strategy kept her safe but also deeply alone. Every time intimacy deepened or conflict arose, her body screamed at her to go. And she'd listen, packing her bags before she even understood what she was running from.

Then there was Daniel, who combined freeze and fawn in a different way than I did. When conflict arose, he'd go completely blank. Not just quiet, but empty. His mind would literally stop working. He'd stand there, unable to access words, thoughts, or feelings. People often mistook it for passive aggression.

"I'm not giving them the silent treatment," he explained, frustrated. "I genuinely can't find myself. It's like I've left my body and I'm watching from somewhere far away."

Daniel had grown up with a parent who would interrogate him about his feelings, demanding explanations he couldn't give. His nervous system had learned that the safest thing to do was to vacate. If he wasn't home, he couldn't give the wrong answer.

Marcus fights. Priya flees. Daniel disappears. I freeze, then fix. Each of us convinced that our response is protecting us. Each of us paying a price we didn't agree to.

None of these responses makes us wrong; they make us profoundly human. Our nervous system is just doing its job—keeping us safe at all costs. When it signals that something doesn't feel safe, this is vital information that needs our attention. We are wired that way for *survival*.

⟁Ask yourself: What does your body tend to do when conflict arises? Fight, flight, freeze, or fawn? Can you trace that back to an environment where that response made sense?

Gaining some insight into your reactions does not mean you are suddenly expected to control them. It simply means starting to notice them when they happen and being curious. With practice, you will become aware of the moment your body steps in and says, "Leave this to me!" even when the situation doesn't require emergency measures.

Noticing creates a crucial shift—from judgment to curiosity, from shame to awareness. Only when we can witness our impulses without self-blame can we begin to choose something different.

The Space Between

When you begin to recognize your patterned impulse in real time, you create a powerful opening. It might be barely visible, but it's meaningful all the same. The urge to react is still there, but you can name it now, and that lays the foundation for change.

Remaining present does not always feel natural when your past experiences have conditioned you to flee or take self-protective action. The moment your system senses danger, it tries to default to your patterned response.

That's why even when you are aware of it, the pull can still be strong. Your job is not to be perfect; it's to pay attention to your body.

⟡Ask yourself: Can you recall a situation where you almost reacted automatically, but something in you held back for a moment? What allowed you to notice it? Did you do anything differently?

We will discuss how to catch opportunities to pause in later chapters, but simply noticing when your body begins to take over can initiate change.

When the Impulse Becomes a Flood

Sometimes we can be blindsided by an emotional trigger, and the patterned reaction is too fast for us to be able to pause. Your breath disappears. Your clarity vanishes. Suddenly, you're gone—hijacked, helpless, and ashamed. This experience is so common that renowned researcher, Dr. John Gottman, gave it a name: *emotional flooding.* He describes it as a state in which your nervous system becomes so overloaded with emotion that your ability to reason and communicate effectively is temporarily shut down. You are not just upset; you have been physiologically overthrown.

You don't choose when you get swept away by the rapids. Your body has remembered a moment when you weren't safe, and it initiates flooding to protect you—to get you as far from danger as quickly as possible, with or without your say-so.

I can recall being in a work meeting where someone asked me a barrage of questions, and I froze. I couldn't think. Eventually, I had to leave the room to allow my heart rate to slow. It wasn't the questions that overwhelmed me; it was the way in which they were asked. The person's voice came at me like rapid fire, and their tone was sharp; to my nervous system, it felt like an attack.

When you are emotionally flooded, your prefrontal cortex—the part of the brain responsible for language, perspective, and regulation—goes offline. The limbic system (emotional center) and brain stem (survival impulses) take over. As a result, you can't think clearly or make conscious choices, and you start reacting instead.

This might look like blanking out, stammering, or saying something you later regret. Before you know it, the conflict is no longer about what's happening now. It's become a spiral of painful thoughts and beliefs: *I'm a terrible person unworthy of being loved, heard, or respected.* The thoughts that surface aren't random; they're echoes of past experiences:

I always mess things up.
They don't want me here.
I'm too much.

Yet in those moments, your thoughts don't feel historical. They feel factual. This is the power of *emotional reasoning*: a cognitive distortion where your mind concludes that something is real simply because it *feels* real. When you're emotionally flooded, your whole system conspires to convince you that what it recognizes as familiar is true, even when it's not.

In those moments, you don't just feel bad; you *are* bad. The whole narrative collapses onto you. Then, the conversation is not about a specific problem or tension. It's about whether or not you are worthy of love, safety, or respect at all. That's what makes it so hard to find your center; the moment has become a referendum on your worth, and when that happens, shame rushes in. Brené Brown's research has shown that shame thrives in silence and secrecy, both of which are created by emotional flooding. You turn inward, you retreat, you stop reaching for support, and the voice inside you gets louder, more rigid, and more absolute.

I have seen this in my clients again and again: intelligent, thoughtful, emotionally attuned people who shut down mid-conflict and later berate themselves for not knowing what to say. I have been there, too. It's humbling, yet deeply human. The more we understand what's happening inside us, the more compassion we can bring to the moments we wish we'd handled differently.

When you're caught in the rapids, the world narrows. Context disappears. You can't remember that the person across from you loves you, or that you are usually good at your job, or that this conversation won't last forever. All you hear is the critical voice in your head.

Flooding can show up as:

Shutting down — You freeze, go quiet, and lose access to your thoughts. You may appear calm but feel a sense of emptiness or a foggy feeling inside.

Overfunctioning — You immediately jump in to fix, smooth over, or take responsibility for everyone's discomfort to end the tension.

Disconnecting — You smile, nod, and perform politeness, but inside, you've already checked out. You are no longer present in the moment.

Becoming explosive — You speak before thinking, escalate quickly, or feel your tone shift before your mind catches up.

What these all have in common is that they aren't deliberate choices. They are your nervous system saying *This is too much* and doing what it has always done to get you through.

Your reaction to emotional flooding is often more about the history that is called forth in those moments—when your body didn't have the time, support, or safety to process what happened— than the present events.

Your nervous system has filed those memories away without words, but not without weight. An event with even a small resonance in the present can activate emotional content that was stored but never fully felt. Your body responds as if the past is happening again, even if your rational mind knows better.

As neuroscientist Lisa Feldman Barrett explains, your *body budget*—which is your system's energy reserves—decreases with stress, making small tensions feel disproportionately large. When your body budget is depleted from a stressful week, your system is on high alert, so a seemingly minor comment can trigger a major impulse.

According to developmental psychologist Allan Schore, repeated early stress can lead to hypersensitivity in the brain's right hemisphere, the part responsible for interpreting facial expressions, tone of voice, and nonverbal social cues. So when someone's voice tightens or they go quiet, you may not notice it, but your system reads it as *danger*, even if your logical mind disagrees.

It's important not to judge yourself for your reactions. Freezing is not a weakness, and you are not "too much" if you flare up. Disappearing when things get hard doesn't mean you're broken. Your body practiced these strategies long before you had words to explain them. The rapids don't come from nowhere. They rise from memory, and sometimes that memory lives only in the body.

♡Ask yourself: When you flood, what does it look like—exploding, freezing, fixing, or fading out? What kinds of moments bring it on fastest? Can you trace back to when that strategy first worked?

When your reaction feels disproportionate, it doesn't mean you are overreacting. It means you are carrying something deeper. That's the strange gift of flooding: It reveals where tenderness still lives.

What to Do in the Face of Impulse

Impulse is the body's first attempt to protect us, and it doesn't need to be erased to be transformed. When we start to notice it with curiosity instead of shame, we begin reclaiming something powerful: the ability to stay with ourselves in the moment, even when things get hard.

A breath of awareness, a two-second pause, a flicker of noticing—these small moments matter. They are the difference between living on autopilot and living with intention. And while impulse may still show up because you are human, how you respond moving forward is no longer just a reaction. It's a choice waiting to be made.

Impulse vs. Habit

While impulse is your nervous system's reflexive, immediate response to perceived threat—happening in a split second, before your brain has time to interpret the moment—habit is what happens next. It's the next move we make once the initial surge passes—a follow-up behavior that feels like a choice but often isn't. It's the behavior you move into once the initial jolt subsides. It feels more deliberate but often is not.

Habit is your second action, for example: overexplaining, apologizing, fixing, or disappearing. These aren't random. They're learned strategies, shaped by repetition and reinforced through neural wiring created by everything that's come before.

The moment you can name your impulse is the moment you stop being owned by it. You can stop reacting and start witnessing.

And in that space between, something new becomes possible. You can begin to create new habits, choosing responses rather than repeating old patterns.

What you've learned in this chapter:
- ***Impulse comes fast, before thought, and is shaped by historic patterns.***
- ***Fight, flight, freeze, or fawn are automatic nervous system reactions.***
- ***These patterns are protective adaptations.***
- ***Flooding happens when past emotional patterns overwhelm you in the present.***

Chapter 3: Habit – The Pattern That Follows

"When an inner situation is not made conscious, it happens outside, as fate." –Carl Jung

Impulse is a flash. Habit is the well-worn groove that follows. It's the next move we make once the initial surge passes—a follow-up behavior that feels like a choice but often isn't. It's a decision influenced by old patterns and trauma.

In my responses to conflict in my relationships, while my impulse was to freeze, my habitual response was to make peace at any cost. The moment I sensed conflict—emotional distance, a sigh, a slight energy shift—I would feel a tightness in my chest in my body, a panicked feeling of shrinking. Once the freeze subsided, habit stepped in, swinging me into a response that seemed opposite to my impulse—I'd overexplain, apologize, and start fixing everything I could think to fix, throwing myself at the other person's needs to close the gap before it widened.

In the example I gave about my response to a coworker yelling at me in front of others, I described freezing, but I didn't explain what happened next. When the adrenaline wore off, my nervous system flipped from freeze to fawn, and I became obsessed with repairing the damage in the relationship. I rewrote emails, asked others for feedback on how I could improve, and stayed late to try to anticipate every possible mistake. This wasn't coming from clarity; it was a full-blown appeasement spiral. I felt I had to earn my way back into being safe, respected, even liked.

Looking back, it was not about that one meeting. It was the legacy habit kicking in: *If I overperform, maybe I won't be punished. Maybe I'll be allowed to stay.* Outwardly, it looked like kindness or care. Internally, it was desperation. The belief behind it was quiet but constant: *If I do everything possible to appease them, I'll be loved.* Strangely, that coworker and most of the people I've tried to appease never noticed, because I didn't make a scene, raise my voice, or do anything dramatic. I just worked harder. Smiled more. Said less. My pattern flew under the radar and was so automatic that I couldn't see it for a long time.

Ask yourself: What does your conflict response habit look like? What's your automatic move after the impulse subsides? Do you start fixing, apologizing, withdrawing, analyzing, blaming, or shrinking?

Looking back, I see it so clearly. It wasn't a one-time thing; it was a loop I repeated in every relationship until therapy helped me name it, trace it back, and interrupt it. For a long time, I couldn't even tell it was a pattern. It felt like love, like doing my part, like keeping the peace. But it wasn't peace. It was self-abandonment cleverly disguised as care.

One of my coaching clients (we'll call her Elena) is the perfect example of this. She was in the middle of a difficult stretch with her ex, trying to co-parent without falling back into old battles. During a call, he rattled off a list of complaints: the kids' routines, their behavior, the calendar, and how everything she did was wrong. What did she do? She began taking notes on what needed to be changed and what *she* needed to fix.

What she did *not* do was speak up for herself.

Instead of expressing how hurt she was, she defaulted to an apology. Then came the offer to take on more responsibility—anything to keep the peace. Even though the conversation felt completely one-sided and unfair, she minimized her feelings, convincing herself that being *the bigger person* was the right thing to do. Later, she told me, "I was proud I didn't explode. But I also felt like I disappeared."

That's the thing about habit. It doesn't always look messy. Sometimes habit appears to be doing the right thing. But if it comes at the cost of your core values and needs, you aren't creating peace; you're just abandoning yourself. While I would never advocate for exploding at someone, I do advocate for acting according to our values. We'll revisit this later in the book.

How Habits Are Formed

In neuroscience terms, an impulse is governed by the brain stem and limbic system, which is quick, emotional, and unconscious. Habit, on the other hand, is often routed through your *Default Mode Network* (DMN), which draws on past experiences and your internalized self-concept to predict what you *should* do next. It's like an overconfident GPS constantly rerouting you using outdated maps of fear and misunderstanding.

The impulse keeps you alive. The habit keeps you accepted.

Conflict habits don't start as habits. They begin as adaptations, responses that helped us feel safe, accepted, or in control at some earlier point in our lives. In a moment of stress, your body reacts quickly, bypassing thought to protect you. If that reaction *works*, your brain makes a mental note: *That helped. Let's remember it.* As neuroscientist Donald Hebb put it, "Neurons that fire together, wire together."

Your brain is the ultimate efficiency expert. If it can automate a response—like your go-to *I'm fine* when you're decidedly *not* fine— it will, patting itself on the back for saving precious energy, even if that efficiency is to your detriment. So, your conflict behaviors get rehearsed over and over until they no longer feel like choices at all. They become automatic and deeply embodied.

In Chapter 2, we met the *firefighter parts* who reactively spring into action to stop overwhelming internal distress and can be somewhat impulsive. Habitual patterns and behaviors are often driven by what Internal Family Systems calls *manager parts*, which proactively work to manage day-to-day life and prevent emotional pain. Managers are usually risk-averse. Concerned only with safety and security, they constantly calculate and orchestrate your responses to maintain a sense of control and avoid potential distress.

Whenever you choose harmony over honesty, silence over assertion, or caretaking over confrontation, you strengthen the connection between that emotional trigger and behavioral response. Over time, it no longer feels like a choice. It just feels like you.

Through a process called *synaptic pruning,* the brain trims away connections that aren't used often and strengthens the ones you return to again and again. That's part of why these responses feel automatic. Repeated experiences strengthen specific neural pathways, making them the brain's go-to response, even when they no longer serve us.

I once worked with a client (we'll call him Jason) who prided himself on being steady under pressure. He wore it like a badge of honor, but in one session, he paused and said, "I don't think I'm calm because I'm grounded. I think I'm calm because I'm terrified of what might happen if I'm not."

That moment was huge.

His calm was freezing, formed in childhood when his father's anger filled the house like smoke. When things got tense, Jason didn't express himself. He disappeared.

He thought it was strength, but it was survival.

These realizations can be really disorienting. You start questioning what you thought was real. And the legacy stored in your nervous system? It's sticky. It does not yield to logic; it requires intention.

These patterns delivered results once in the form of connection, approval, or survival. They earned love—or at least they avoided loss. But they come with a quiet cost: yourself.

⟲Ask yourself: What's one "calm" behavior you tend to default to after conflict starts to settle? If you trace it back, when did it first begin? What might your nervous system be trying to protect you from when you do it?

It's hard to notice our habits because they often don't feel like a response we can choose. They become so automatic that they start to feel like a part of your personality, even though they're simply a form of protection. Often, these habits begin in households where silence, fixing, or caretaking kept you connected or made you feel safe. With the help of this book, you can consciously interrupt these deeply ingrained strategies, build new pathways, and repattern them.

Without ever signing up for it, we inherit an emotional blueprint—an internal map etched by the dynamics of our early relationships, shaped by what was allowed, what was punished, and what was simply not noticed. While genetics has a powerful influence on our biology, our early relationships shape this emotional blueprint. We carry forward not only our DNA but also the invisible choreography of roles we were unconsciously trained to perform to stay connected to our caregivers, especially when love felt conditional.

During childhood, we learn which emotions are acceptable and which ones get punished. We learn who gets to take up space and who does not. We learn the subtle rules of belonging, and we follow them, even decades later, without realizing we're still playing by the same rules.

Some of us became useful to be loved. Others learned that shrinking keeps the peace. Some stayed strong to avoid becoming a burden on others.

These patterns are not automatically relinquished with age. IFS theory helps clarify the nature of these childhood adaptations—how the strategies that once kept us safe can later limit our emotional freedom. For example, when a child learns to suppress their needs to take care of a volatile parent or becomes the *responsible one* while everyone else falls apart, those strategies often endure into adulthood. They become the lens through which you interpret conflict and the compass that guides your behavior when things get hard.

That compass does not always point toward the truth. It points toward what once felt safe.

Attachment theory supports this idea, showing that our earliest bonds with caregivers shape relational patterns that often persist into adulthood. The ways we learned to stay safe in relationships do not vanish with age. If love once meant self-sacrifice, we keep offering ourselves up, even when no one is asking. If speaking up once brought punishment or distance, we quiet ourselves time and again, confusing fear for composure. If you learned that love required self-sacrifice, you'll keep sacrificing, even when no one's asking you to. If speaking up got you punished or ignored, you might default to silence, thinking it's a sign of stoicism, when it's just fear in disguise.

One client (we'll call him Alex) always avoided confrontation with his partner. He wouldn't push back, admit he was hurt, or say when something didn't feel right. "I just want to be the calm one," he said. When we traced that pattern back, we uncovered the fear behind the calm. In his childhood home, disagreements exploded into days-long fights. His nervous system had learned that speaking up came at too high a cost.

What he thought was virtue was actually avoidance—a survival strategy masquerading as composure.

The heartbreaking part is how often these inherited responses are praised! "You are so mature, so chill, and so good at keeping the peace."

Ask yourself: What "strengths" do others praise you for? Your calm, your kindness, your reliability, which may have started as protection? What might those patterns be costing you now?

Watch for Praise That Feeds the Pattern

Not all compliments are neutral. For years, I loved being called "reliable" until I realized that reliability was just the pretty name for my fear of disappointing anyone.

If you are constantly praised for being the calm one, the flexible one, or the one who holds it together, ask yourself: *Am I being seen for who I am, or for the role I trained myself to play?*

The first step is seeing it clearly. These legacy loops are like a catchy pop song, impossible to get out of your head—except instead of a catchy tune, I had a deeply ingrained belief that if I didn't immediately fix a problem, I was failing.

To break free, I had to see the loop. I couldn't just feel bad about it; I had to map it out.

After a conflict left me feeling activated and ashamed, I would sit down and retrace my steps to see the pattern from a distance. It was like drawing a map of my autopilot.

I invite you to try the reflection that I used.

⟳ *Workbook Moment: Map Your Autopilot Loop*

Think of a recent conflict that activated you. Walk yourself through this reflection:

1. **Impulse**: What happened in your body first? (Tightness in chest, heat in face, going blank, urge to fix.)
2. **Habit**: What did you do? (Stayed quiet? Got defensive? Smoothed things over?)
3. **Belief**: What story did your brain tell you afterward? *(I messed up again. They don't respect me. I can't do this.)*
4. **Identity**: What do you assume about yourself in conflict? *(I'm too emotional. I always get it wrong. I can't handle tension.)*

Now ask yourself: *Are these facts, or rehearsed interpretations?*

The Hidden Cost of Getting Stuck

There's a kind of exhaustion that doesn't come from doing too much but from continuing to do what no longer serves you. You feel empty inside. This is the weariness of self-betrayal. Most of the time, it goes unnoticed because it doesn't scream. It simmers.

Legacy patterns don't just shape your behavior; they shape your identity. But over time, even the most polished roles can begin to chafe. You might still be doing all the right things, but you feel more and more disconnected from your true Self.

This dissonance is subtle. It's the quiet ache after a conversation where you didn't speak your truth. It's the resentment you feel when your needs are once again deprioritized. And then, there's the voice in your head that finally names part of the problem: *Why am I always the one adjusting? When is it my turn?*

Often, no one else sees the cost, but you feel it—in your body. In your spirit. In your aliveness.

One of my clients, Kara, found herself in this exact situation. She kept giving her partner chance after chance. He always said the right things: "I'm working on it," "I'll do better next time," "You mean the world to me." She desperately wanted to believe him. But her nervous system had learned, early and deeply, that love had to be earned, that consistency was rare, and crumbs were better than nothing. So she clung to those crumbs.

Her voice was steady when she talked about it, but her hands stayed clenched in her lap. "I want to believe him," she said, "but something always feels missing, and I keep pretending I don't notice."

The gap between his words and actions grew wider. He kept showing up late, dismissing her feelings, and breaking promises. With each disappointment, something in her twisted tighter, a knot of confusion, self-doubt, and shame that she couldn't seem to unravel.

Why do we hold on so long, even when it hurts? It's not weakness or foolishness; it's our wiring. If you grew up in a household where love was inconsistent or had to be earned, your nervous system might confuse chaos for care. You learned to read between the lines, to chase those little "crumbs" of affection. So when this partner offered a breadcrumb in the form of an apology or a tender moment, her hope would surge. The hope would continually persist: *Maybe this time will be different.* Over time, though, the same cycle repeated, leaving her feeling emptier and more invisible.

This is the hidden cost of waiting for someone to become who they could be. We lose touch with who we are. We trade clarity for fantasy, boundaries for longing, and self-trust for the illusion of control.

As Kara admitted in a session, "I don't even want him back. I just want him to finally be the man he promised to be. I feel like I can't rest until that happens." That is the hook of hope, but not the kind that lifts you. It's the kind that tethers you to disappointment.

Kara and I worked together for almost a year. It took her six months to finally see the pattern clearly, and another three to do something about it.

She didn't leave her partner in one dramatic moment. She left in inches. First, she stopped making excuses for him to her friends. Then she stopped making excuses to herself. She started documenting the gap between his words and his actions—not to punish him, but to anchor herself in reality when her hope tried to distort it.

The breaking point came on a Tuesday night when he forgot they had plans. Again. She sat in the restaurant alone for forty minutes, and somewhere in that waiting, something shifted. She wasn't angry. She was done.

"I realized I was waiting for him to become someone he'd already shown me he wasn't," she told me in our next session. "And every day I stayed, I was choosing his potential over my peace."

She moved out the following month. It wasn't graceful or painless. She second-guessed herself constantly. She missed him, or missed the version of him she'd constructed in her mind. But she also noticed something surprising: Her shoulders dropped. Her sleep improved. The knot in her stomach that she'd carried for two years started to loosen.

Last I heard, she was living alone for the first time in her adult life. Learning to trust her own judgment again. Building a relationship with herself that didn't require anyone else's validation.

Kara's story doesn't end with a new, better partner. It ends with her choosing herself. Sometimes that's the whole story.

Another client, Eric, intellectualized every argument. He was calm, articulate, and always reasonable, but almost too reasonable. During one session, he described a recent fight with his partner. His words were polished, even insightful, but his shoulders stayed tense, and he didn't meet my eyes.

"I don't yell. I don't shut her down," he said. "I just try to stay logical." Underneath the logic was fear. Raised in a chaotic household where shouting quickly turned to chaos, Eric had learned to stay safe by detaching. Emotion, to him, felt dangerous.

Over time, that detachment turned into disconnection. He could handle any crisis except vulnerability. "I'm great in emergencies," he admitted with a tight smile, "but I don't know how to be in intimacy."

The cost of such disconnection accumulates quietly over time. You don't collapse. Instead, you erode. This slow erosion may show up as the weight of all the emotional labor you never signed up for but assumed anyway. Or maybe it's the slow leak of self-trust as you keep deferring to others, doubting your instincts, and choosing comfort for others over clarity for yourself.

Eventually, this accumulated stress from being misaligned with ourselves will manifest in our bodies. As Bessel van der Kolk reminds us, the body keeps the score. Whether it's chronic stress, inflammation, or illness, the toll of living out of alignment is unmistakable, even if it is rarely visible to others.

⟳Ask yourself: What emotional labor are you still doing out of habit? What do you keep taking on, silently, automatically, that no longer feels true? How would it feel to ask, even just internally: What if I didn't?

That's the question that signals readiness to begin living from a place that is true for *you.*

Before You Can Choose Differently

A few years ago, I got a message from a family member that left me stunned. It was full of accusations: false, exaggerated, even absurd. I remember my heart racing as I read it, my fingers already typing out a reply before I could take a breath. I thought I was responding calmly. I tried to explain, to correct, to clarify the misunderstanding carefully. On the surface, it looked like a measured response, but looking back, I know I was not grounded. I was scared.

The fear was below the surface. I was able to see it only after a few sessions with my therapist. I was terrified of being misunderstood, of being abandoned, if I didn't fix it right away. The effort to quiet that frantic need to repair, to resolve, to get things back under control was not a choice I was making in that moment. It was a pattern—one I'd been repeating for years. Even though my response was kind, it did not quite communicate what I really needed. What I needed was space, a face-to-face conversation, or maybe the courage to say, *This hurt, and I don't know how to answer right now.* None of those honest responses felt available to me at the time, because my nervous system had already made up its mind: explain. Soften. Make it okay. Do *anything* to feel safe.

That's the cost of living from a legacy script. You might get through the conversation without an explosion, or you might even feel proud of your composure, but somewhere inside, a quieter part of you knows that *there is a deeper truth you haven't prioritized.*

When we start to separate our truth from our training, we start to reclaim our lives. We interrupt not only the first reflex, but the habit that follows close behind, the one that's so familiar it feels like us. We start asking new questions: *What actually matters here? What's true for me? What am I trying to protect?* When we do, something starts to shift. Over time, we stop defaulting to the version of ourselves that kept the peace at any cost. We start becoming the version that tells the truth—gently, but unapologetically.

The question now isn't about how to go back and fix the past, but about how to stop letting your legacy patterns and self-limiting beliefs covertly run the show. To answer that, we need to explore what becomes possible when we see the script and choose not to follow it. That's where we go next: into the practice of creating the space where a new kind of response becomes available.

What you've learned in this chapter:
- *Habit is your second response, the role you slide into after the initial jolt.*
- *These patterns (overexplaining, pleasing, disappearing) often look like strengths.*
- *Legacy roles are rehearsed in families and rewarded socially.*
- *Every small pause you create weakens the grip of the legacy response.*

Chapter 4: The Exhale–Explore–Engage Method

"The most common way people give up their power is by thinking they don't have any." –Alice Walker

By now, if you've been reading with an open heart and a willing body, you've probably begun to notice things you hadn't quite seen before—patterns so familiar they blend into the background. You may start to notice that you go quiet in moments that matter, the way your voice sharpens when you feel unheard, or the way you try to fix things quickly because of the unbearable discomfort of not knowing what will happen next. These are the patterns that live just below the surface, shaping your days, your relationships, and your sense of Self, often without your conscious consent.

We have explored emotional flooding, when those fast, instinctive reactions come to life. We talked about how your body reacts long before your brain has a chance to weigh in. You learned that what may seem like overreacting is your nervous system replaying an unfinished story—a moment of overwhelm that was stored away before it could be felt or understood. You realized that being flooded is not a failure—it's a flare, a signal, your body's way of helping you through moments that feel unsafe because they echo ones that once were.

Then we looked at how that first wave settles into quieter but equally powerful old habits; these are often orchestrated by your manager parts—when you silence yourself out of fear, overexplain, appease, or simply disappear. Habits may be harder to see because the way you show up in these moments—outwardly composed or trying to make things right—is often rewarded socially. Yet when you walk away from a moment that looks fine on the outside while feeling a hollow ache on the inside, that's a sign that the version of you that took care of things might have kept the peace, but at the cost of something essential.

That version of yourself does not reflect your truth. That's your training, and we traced where that training comes from: the roles you learned to play in your family, the messages you absorbed about what it means to be good, safe, lovable. These are the ways your parts adapted beautifully to difficult situations, and it is precisely these patterns that the journey of repatterning aims to address, freeing you from paying their price long after they are needed. We also discussed neuroscience, noting that these patterns aren't just emotional; they are physical neural pathways formed through repetition, refined by survival, and reinforced by every moment when choosing differently felt too risky, too strange, or too far out of reach.

You've seen by now how these two forces, impulse and habit, can pull you in opposite directions and still land you in the same place: feeling like you didn't quite get to show up as the version of yourself you are trying to grow into. Sometimes it's because you acted too fast. At other times it's because you played it too safe. Either way, the outcome is the same: regret, self-doubt, and a sense that something is still not right.

Maybe you've also seen how deeply human these responses to conflict are. We respond the way we do not because we are broken or incapable of change, but because of a lifetime of strategies that once made sense.

You may be beginning to notice the gap between your first instinct and your deeper values, sensing that calm does not always indicate you are honoring your truth and that quiet does not always reflect wisdom.

You may have been aware of instances in which keeping the peace with others did not leave you with a sense of inner peace but may have come at the cost of your voice, your truth, or your well-being.

You may be beginning to wonder what might be possible if you could stay in the discomfort just long enough to find your authentic voice—not the one trained to soothe others or prove your worth, but the one that knows what matters most and how to honor it.

That wondering is what brought you here.

Now it's time to walk through the Exhale–Explore–Engage Method step by step.

The Cost of Not Choosing Differently

Most of us aren't walking through life thinking, *I'm going to ignore my truth today.* We're trying to be kind and cooperative, good members of society. We tell ourselves we're being mature, that we're making the best of things, and maybe we are. However, if we look just a little closer—if we quiet ourselves enough to listen to what lies beneath the surface of the rationalizations—something else is often happening.

We're shape-shifting.

We're holding our breath and smiling through discomfort, offering patience when what we feel is anger, apologizing for things we didn't do, or staying silent when something important needs to be said. While it might look like we're "doing the right thing," the body keeps track of what we're giving up in the process.

I later came across a name for that feeling; Martha Beck called it *integrity snarl*. That name perfectly captured my experience: that inner tangle when my actions contradicted what I knew to be true. I looked like I was "put together" on the outside, but on the inside, I felt myself starting to fray.

That feeling wasn't only in my head; I felt it in my body. It was around that time I started reading everything I could about mind-body medicine, and the pieces finally began to click into place. I read books that explained how living out of alignment, swallowing my truth, and chronic stress could lead to real physical consequences: inflammation, hormonal imbalance, and a weakened immune system. It wasn't new-age fluff. It was my life. The body doesn't lie, even when *we* try to.

Lissa Rankin's research on mind-body medicine confirms what many of us have already felt: When we live out of alignment with our truth, our bodies suffer. Reading her book *Mind Over Medicine* felt like another key turning a lock I didn't know was there. I learned how things like chronic stress and constantly swallowing my feelings weren't only emotional burdens; they could activate the body's stress response, leading to real, physical issues like inflammation and a weakened immune system.

It was a startling realization: When I ignored what my body knew, when I kept saying "yes" to things that felt like a "no," my nervous system was screaming out loud what my voice had been swallowing. For me, this showed up as a recurring, tension-fueled migraine that would appear after particularly draining work weeks where I'd smiled through meetings, acting agreeable when I actually disagreed. My body was sending a clear invoice for the peace I had pretended to keep.

And it doesn't end there. Our relationships suffer, too. When we respond from old patterns, we often think we're preserving connection, but what we're actually preserving is a performance.

One of my clients once told me, "I have been the 'easy one' my whole life. I thought that made me lovable, but now I realize it just made me invisible." She had spent years saying the right things, doing what was expected, managing other people's emotions so well that no one ever saw hers. On the surface, her relationships were peaceful, but inside, she felt chronically unseen.

Another client, a leader in a high-pressure workplace, took pride in being composed in every meeting. "I never let anyone see me sweat," she said, "but I also never said what I thought." She had traded authenticity for safety, and it left her team confused and her creativity blocked. When we dug deeper, she realized her "neutrality" was a freeze response, one that started in childhood and had followed her into the boardroom.

These are the stories I hear over and over from people with big hearts and good intentions who've spent years responding to conflict by disappearing just a little. While the cost is not always visible, it's real.

It shows up in the exhaustion that doesn't make sense, in the friendships that feel one-sided, the marriage that feels too polite, the job that looks perfect on paper but drains the color from your life. It shows up in the quiet ache that follows when you abandon yourself for the sake of harmony. At some point, you've done it for so long that eventually it starts to feel like *you*.

That's how legacy works; it dresses up as maturity, responsibility, and kindness. It tells you that being *too much, too direct*, or *too honest* will ruin everything.

So you keep the peace. You minimize your needs. You make yourself easier to love, and slowly, the life you've built starts to reflect everyone's expectations but your own.

The time has come to realign with your truth and repattern your responses. Your vitality depends on it.

Before we dive into the practice itself, I want to offer a moment of reflection:

♡Ask yourself: Where in your life have you been managing instead of living? What would it feel like to be seen, heard, and held not for your performance, but for your presence?

What Becomes Possible

When you repattern and start living from your truth, something subtle but profound begins to shift. Saying *no* from a place of self-permission signals this change. You'll experience it by staying present in difficult conversations to express yourself authentically, without reverting to old patterns of guilt or the need for external validation. This fundamentally alters your relationships: Connections that leave you depleted will find equilibrium, those in which you don't feel fully accepted may fade, and authentic relationships will deepen on a foundation of genuine, rather than performative, connection.

Perfection is not the goal. Old patterns will still surface, and the impulses to appease, defend, control, or retreat won't vanish entirely. The difference is that they will no longer dictate your actions because you've cultivated a space—a significant pause— where your truth can reside.

Through consistent effort, the gap between a trigger and a clear understanding will lessen. Your inner space will become more tranquil, freeing you from being entangled in every reaction and fostering self-trust. This trust does not stem from always being right but from knowing you'll remain present, even amidst difficulty, and that you'll show up consistently.

Clients tell me constantly that learning to use this framework not only helped them navigate conflict but also gave them back pieces of themselves they hadn't even realized were missing.

One woman said, "I feel like I stopped performing and started participating in my own life." Another told me she finally understood what it meant to feel emotionally safe with others and with herself.

This kind of work changes the trajectory of a life because, once you know how to **Exhale, Explore,** and **Engage** with awareness, you can meet any moment with presence and move through conflict without abandoning yourself. You can look back on your choices with pride, knowing they were truly yours.

I want to take a moment here to reassure you that *this process is not linear, and the timeline is not predictable.* And if you hit some bumps in the road, that's a good sign that you've taken the courage to experiment and are brave enough to try a different way of living.

Some of you will feel shifts within weeks. Others will practice for months and still find themselves reverting to old patterns when stress spikes. Both are normal. Both are part of the work.

Change doesn't announce itself with fanfare. More often, it sneaks up on you. You'll be mid-conflict and suddenly notice your breath. You'll catch yourself about to appease... and then you'll pause instead. You'll speak a truth that used to terrify you and realize your voice didn't shake. Don't dismiss these moments as being small. They're everything.

There will also be setbacks. Days when you react exactly how you always have and then feel the familiar crush of disappointment. Weeks when the gap between who you want to be and who you are in the moment feels unbridgeable. These aren't failures. They're the nonlinear reality of rewiring a nervous system that's been practicing these patterns for decades.

Some relationships will deepen as you become more authentic.

Other people in your life will struggle with your new boundaries and changing patterns. A few relationships may not survive your transformation. This isn't a sign you're doing it wrong. It's a sign you're doing it *for real*.

Real change lives in the practice—in the sometimes messy, often repetitive work of catching yourself, pausing, choosing differently, failing, and then trying again. This book gives you the tools and framework, but the power of lasting change comes from your commitment to keep practicing.

What I can promise is this: **If you stay with the practice, something will shift**. Maybe not in the timeline you'd hoped for. Maybe not in the way you expect. But the version of you who stays present in hard moments, who speaks their truth without cruelty, who honors your own needs while remaining connected to others? That version of you isn't fantasy—they're already inside you, waiting for enough practice to emerge.

Ask yourself: Where in your life would it mean everything to trust yourself more? What relationship, conversation, or decision would shift if you had the tools to stay with your truth instead of falling into your legacy patterns?

The Exhale–Explore–Engage Method

For years, I felt as though my reactions owned me. I'd get hijacked, saying or doing things that didn't feel like me, and then spend hours picking apart everything I'd said or done. I needed a way to interrupt that spiral—something simple I could remember in the heat of the moment before I disappeared inside myself.

Slowly, through trial and a lot of error, I found a sequence that worked. It was a lifeline. It always started with my breath. I learned that before I could do anything else, I had to **Exhale**. The purpose was simply to interrupt the automatic response, to ask myself, *What's happening in my body right now?*

Just one conscious breath gave me enough space to **Explore**. I could get curious about the story my brain was telling me and trace the reaction back to its root. I would ask, *Where is this feeling coming from?* Only then, from that place of clarity, could I choose how to **Engage**. Engaging wasn't about finding the perfect response; it was about finding the one that felt true to me.

Exhale. Explore. Engage. This was a way back to myself. It became my map out of the fog.

What you've learned in this chapter:
- *A different choice exists in the space between your default reaction and the recognition that you don't have to respond that way.*
- *Impulse and habit are not personality; they are patterns.*
- *Discomfort is often the first sign of real change. If it feels unfamiliar, you are probably doing it right.*
- *Your nervous system can be repatterned to learn to trust slower, more accurate responses.*
- *You don't have to rewrite your story all at once. You can make one new choice at a time.*

Chapter 5: Exhale – Feel the Shift

"When you own your breath, nobody can steal your peace."
–Unknown

I used to think that the moment a conflict started, the story was already written. The ending felt inevitable. Whether it was across the table from my husband, the air thick with unspoken words, or in a tense meeting at work, my reaction was always a flash of heat. My body would brace, my mind would race, and I'd already be three steps down a path of defending, fixing, or freezing. There was no space between the spark and the explosion.

So the idea that I could find a pause in that storm felt like a fantasy. A breath? A moment of stillness? To me, that sounded like surrender. It felt like letting the other person win, or worse—like allowing a wave of shame to crash over me without a fight. My body was trained for speed, for survival. Pausing felt like the most dangerous thing in the world.

But by daring to try and find that impossible moment—that one, single breath—everything began to change.

For me, the change started there: in that subtle interruption of my old script. It was the moment when, instead of letting the emotional current sweep me into another reaction or pull me down the smooth grooves of my legacy patterns, I was able to remember that I had a body, a breath, and a choice. I learned it wasn't about performance; it was about presence. And for me, presence always began with that one breath.

It couldn't be the kind of breath I took automatically, unconsciously, while my mind barreled ahead. It had to be the kind I chose deliberately—the kind that brought me back into myself. It was a breath that slowed things down to disrupt the momentum of a thousand rehearsed responses.

I discovered that when I exhaled on purpose, I wasn't merely calming my nervous system; I was reclaiming the moment. I was letting my body signal to my mind: I can do something differently now.

This intentional breath was my access to what I later learned through Internal Family Systems is called Self-energy—my core of calm, curiosity, and clarity. It was the only state that allowed me to observe my reactive parts, like my inner firefighters, without being consumed by their urgency. It was my only path to responding from a place of wholeness.

I had to be honest with myself. This new way of being went against everything I was trained to do. I was raised in a family and culture that rewarded speed, certainty, and control. I had learned to speak fast, fix quickly, and hold it all in. Pausing felt dangerous because my childhood had taught me that slowness equaled vulnerability and silence invited criticism. I knew that learning to exhale amid conflict wouldn't be easy. It felt radical.

What I started to realize, though, was that the first breath I chose on purpose was the beginning of the entire method taking root in my life. It wasn't the solution—not yet—but it was my refusal to be swept away.

It was my first quiet act of resistance against the old scripts that told me to perform, please, or disappear. That single breath was my first vote for a different future.

And it didn't always feel good. At first, pausing simply felt like failure, like freezing, or losing ground. I'd second-guess myself, feel foolish, exposed, or even guilty for not reacting the way I usually did.

I learned that this discomfort was part of the rewiring process. I was interrupting a pattern that had once kept me safe, and my body noticed. It therefore tried to pull me back to what was familiar, even if it was painful. This wasn't a weakness; it was biology.

Still, with each deliberate breath, I taught my nervous system that presence was possible. I didn't need to rush toward resolution or retreat into silence. I could sit, even briefly, in the space between a trigger and my response, and let something truer emerge. This became my moment of power. It was the moment I remembered that I am not merely a collection of triggers and habits. I am someone who can choose.

I started to think of all the moments when I'd rushed to respond, when my mouth had moved faster than my heart. I thought about what it had cost me, and what might have shifted, inside and outside, if only I had taken that one conscious breath.

⟡Ask yourself: Think of a moment when you rushed to respond, and your mouth moved faster than your heart. What did it cost you? What might have shifted, inside or outside, if you had taken just one conscious breath before acting?

The Physiology of the Pause

If the Exhale–Explore–Engage Method begins with a breath, then it's worth understanding what that breath does *biologically*. Even though the pause may feel small or soft, it is a profoundly active state of regulation. Of interruption. Of quiet rebellion against the nervous system's rush to survive rather than discern.

Your body is exquisitely designed to respond to a threat. When something feels off, such as tone, timing, or tension in the room, your sympathetic nervous system kicks in. Your heart rate increases, your breath becomes shallow, and your muscles tense. That's your body preparing to protect you with fight, flee, fawn, or freeze. It does not wait for your conscious approval. It acts fast.

However, *you can communicate with your body* through your breath. One long exhale is often all it takes to begin that shift.

Why? Because while quick, shallow inhales signal danger and activate the sympathetic nervous system, slow, extended exhales stimulate the *parasympathetic nervous system,* specifically the *vagus nerve.*

That's the branch of your body that governs rest, digestion, and repair. It's the part of your nervous system that says, *You are safe now.* When you access it, even briefly, your brain receives the message: *We don't need to run. We don't need to shut down. We can stay here.*

This is what Stephen Porges' *polyvagal theory* explains so powerfully. It's not only *whether* your nervous system is activated, but *how*—and whether it believes connection is possible. A slow breath can bring you back from shutdown, from hypervigilance, from that rising wave of urgency that feels impossible to ride. It's not magic, it's physiology. And it works.

Neuroscientist Dan Siegel refers to this shift as *moving from reactivity to receptivity*, a space where empathy and clear thinking can return. It's what allows you to choose how you would like to *respond*.

In his work on *mindsight,* Siegel explains that bringing attention to the breath activates the prefrontal cortex, the part of the brain responsible for empathy, insight, and emotional regulation. It literally makes you more capable of seeing yourself and the person across from you with compassion rather than as a threat.

Remember, the pause is subtle. Often invisible. It may not look like anything is happening, but inside, everything is.

You are inserting a space between the trigger and the action. You are catching the wave before it crashes. You are doing the slow, steady work of changing the channel from automatic to intentional.

When you do this enough, that pause becomes easier to find. It stops feeling like a detour and starts becoming a doorway—one that opens into choice.

⊘Ask yourself: How do you know when your body has started to take over in conflict? What are the signs—physical, emotional, or behavioral—that tell you your system is speeding up or shutting down? What does it feel like, physically, to come back into yourself?

Why We Skip the Breath

You'd think something as simple as remembering to extend the breath—to exhale—would be easy to do. A breath, after all, is free, ever-present, and built into your body. But in the very moments we need it most, we override the breath. We abandon it in favor of the reaction.

Why? Because pausing is not just physiological; it's *psychological*. For many people, stillness does not feel safe. It feels like surrender, like exposure, like letting the other person get a step ahead—like losing before you've engaged. Especially if your childhood taught you that slowness equals vulnerability, silence invites criticism, or reacting first was a form of protection, the idea of stopping, even for a breath, can feel unbearable.

The breath is also where the truth lives, something many of us have been trained to avoid. When you stop and breathe, you *feel*. You might notice your heart pounding, a tightness in your chest, or a lump in your throat.

Sometimes it's easier to keep talking, fixing, or performing than to feel the wave rising underneath all that effort. Pausing means being with what's there—and what's there can be overwhelming. I remember trying to pause during a tense financial discussion with my ex-husband. The moment I stopped talking, a wave of pure panic hit me. My inner critic screamed that if I weren't actively defending my position, I would be taken advantage of. The silence felt more dangerous than the argument itself.

One of my clients (I'll call her Rhea) was a master at staying composed. She was raised to be the gracious one, the peacemaker, the one who makes things right. In our sessions, the second she paused to breathe, her eyes filled with tears. "I hate this part," she said. "The moment I breathe, I start crying. So I just keep going instead."

For her, breathing was not a neutral act. It was the gateway to a grief she hadn't let herself feel in decades. That's the hidden cost of skipping the breath: We stay disconnected from ourselves.

There is a deeper consequence, as well. When we don't pause, we reinforce the message that our impulses are urgent and true, that whatever we feel in the moment must be acted on immediately. We miss the chance to *witness* ourselves. To ask, *Is this really me?* or *Is this really what I want to say?* Instead, we ride the wave of reactivity until it crashes, often on someone we love. The breath interrupts that loop, but only if we let it.

⟳Ask yourself: When have you skipped the pause and later wished you hadn't? What would it have taken in that moment to give yourself even just five seconds of stillness? What do you fear might have happened if you hadn't responded right away?

Feel the Shift

It's one thing to understand the *idea* of pausing, but I quickly learned it was useless without a concrete way to practice it in the moment. When my chest got tight and my mind went blank, I needed something to hold onto, an anchor in the storm. Over time, I developed a simple sequence that became that anchor. It's what I return to even now. I want to share the exact steps with you because this is what truly made the difference for me.

I call it *feeling the shift.*

Practice: Feel the Shift

Before the thought, the story, or the urge to fix, flee, or lash out takes over, there is a palpable shift—a subtle moment when something inside you changes. Perhaps your chest tightens, your jaw clenches, your shoulders rise, or your breath disappears altogether. You don't need to understand what triggered it; you just need to notice it. That moment, when your body speaks before your brain catches up, is the doorway to making a choice.

Most of us were never taught to pay attention to this moment. We were taught to override it, suppress it, or push through. We learned to prioritize performance over presence.

What if the shift in your body was not a problem to solve, but an invitation to slow down and stay? What if you could meet that sensation not with fear or urgency, but with awareness and breath?

Feel the Shift invites you to *practice presence*—being present in a way that keeps you rooted in your body long enough to interrupt the autopilot and begin to make a different choice. This is not about fixing your feelings or forcing calm. It's about anchoring yourself in the reality of this moment before the pattern takes hold.

Here is how you do it.

Step 1: Notice sensations in your body

What is happening in my body? Where do I feel this?

Before you can do anything differently, you have to know what's happening in your body. This step involves shifting your attention inward, gently and without judgment, to catch the moment your nervous system begins to activate.

Most of us live in our heads, especially during conflict. We race through thoughts, analyze every word, or mentally draft three possible responses while still pretending to listen. Meanwhile, your body is already speaking. It's saying, *Something doesn't feel right.*

The sooner you can tune into that signal, the more choice you'll have about what happens next. Start small. Don't try to scan your entire body all at once. Instead, pick one area, your chest, your jaw, your hands, your gut, and simply ask: *What do I feel here right now?* Is there tightness? Heat? Numbness? Fluttering? A lump in your throat? You don't need to explain it. Just name the sensation, and allow yourself to feel it for a moment.

Here are a few ways to help yourself notice:

- **Try a body sweep.** Close your eyes and move your attention slowly from head to toe, pausing in places that feel charged or blank.

o **Use a body map.** Mentally draw the outline of your body. Where are you gripping? Holding? Avoiding?

o **Label the sensation with neutral language.** For example: *pressure in my chest, tingling in my hands, buzzing behind my eyes.* Try to describe what it feels like in your body.

o **Put your hand where it hurts (or hums).** Sometimes placing a hand on your chest or stomach brings just enough attention and warmth to make the sensation more accessible.

When you do this, you build a relationship with your body that remembers more than your mind does and speaks volumes if you learn to listen to it.

Why it matters: This kind of noticing interrupts the autopilot response and begins to rewire your relationship with your internal cues. It activates the insular cortex, the part of the brain responsible for internal sensing, and helps reestablish the feedback loop between sensation and awareness. The more quickly you can catch the shift, the more power you have to stay present in that moment.

Step 2: Come back to the present moment

Can I return to the present moment, just a little?

Once you've noticed the shift, the next move is simple but powerful: Come back just enough to remind yourself that you are here, in this moment, and not wherever your nervous system just tried to send you. In conflict, our attention often rushes ahead or spirals back. We replay past conversations or imagine worst-case outcomes—but your body can only live in the present, and that's where your power to choose lives, too.

Returning to the present does not mean becoming totally calm or centered; it simply means reorienting yourself. Find something solid, sensory, and real to ground your awareness in. It might be the sensation of your feet on the floor, the texture of your clothing, the sound of a bird outside, or the hum of a heater in the background. These details don't fix the situation. They anchor you inside it.

Here are a few ways to practice this kind of micro-grounding:

- **Touch something textured.** The edge of your sleeve. The arm of your chair. The fabric of your pants. Let the sensation remind you: *I'm here.*
- **Name three sensory details out loud or in your mind.** For example: *I hear traffic. I feel cool air on my skin. I smell coffee.*
- **Press your feet into the ground.** Notice the contact. Shift your weight slightly. Let gravity hold you.
- **Slowly move your fingers or rotate your shoulders.** Small movements that say, *I'm not frozen. I have agency here.*

Sometimes simply doing one of these things can help shift your internal state by a few degrees. Sometimes it does not. But even the act of trying interrupts the cascade of reactivity enough to give you a breath of space.

Why it matters: Coming back to your body creates a physiological interruption in your stress response. It activates the parasympathetic nervous system, the part of the nervous system responsible for shifting from a state of survival to one of presence. When you bring your attention to your senses, you are letting your system know: *It's okay not to fight or flee right now. We're safe enough to stay present.* From that place, something new becomes possible.

Step 3: Breathe

Can I slow down the breath?

You've noticed the shift. You've anchored yourself in the moment. Now comes the part that might sound overly simple, yet it is anything but: *breathe.*

Breathing is not a quick fix, and it's not about forcing yourself to relax. It's about shifting the conditions inside your body just enough that your nervous system can consider a different option. The goal is not calm; it's contact. You are using your breath to stay with yourself while intense feelings move through you.

Start with one gentle inhale through your nose. Then exhale slowly through your mouth, as if sighing. Do it again. Let each breath remind your system: *I'm here. I'm still with you. We're okay.*

If you feel like your breath is stuck or you can't catch it, try this:

o **Purse your lips on the exhale.** Let the breath stream out like you're blowing through a straw.

o **Count it out.** Inhale for a count of four, then exhale for a count of six. Let the longer exhale guide you back.

o **Pair the breath with a phrase.** Inhale: *This is hard.* Exhale: *I can stay with it.*

The breath is always available, but it's often the first thing we abandon when stress shows up. When you choose to return to it, even briefly, you shift the internal state that, without your pause, would accelerate toward reactivity.

Why it matters: Longer, slower exhales stimulate the vagus nerve, which is the command center of your parasympathetic nervous system. This helps regulate your heart rate, lowers your blood pressure, and signals safety to your entire system. It widens your window of tolerance, the nervous system's capacity for staying present with discomfort while still making a choice. You don't need five minutes of perfect breathing. Sometimes just one conscious exhale is enough to change the moment.

♡Ask yourself: What would it feel like to let your breath guide you through the next hard moment—not to fix it, but to stay connected to yourself inside it?

The moment you pause, something subtle but profound happens. You step off the conveyor belt of your reactions. You loosen the grip of your nervous system's script. You give yourself one breath of space—just enough to remember that there is more to you than the pull to fix, flee, fight, or please. This is not solely about self-regulation. It's about self-remembrance.

When you pause, even briefly, you send yourself a message that the world taught you to forget: *I matter. My experience matters. I don't have to disappear to make this moment safe.*

Of course the urge doesn't vanish merely because you breathe. The legacy patterns don't dissolve in one pause, but something changes. You are no longer on autopilot. From here, something new can begin.

This is the first step of the method: **Exhale.** By taking a breath, you are reclaiming space between impulse and action. That space is yours, and inside it lives a different kind of power, not forceful, not loud, but deeply alive. Stay with your discomfort long enough to choose a response that reflects who you are becoming rather than your history.

What comes next is where the real transformation begins. Once you've taken that breath, once you've interrupted the cycle and accessed your Self-energy, a crucial question emerges from that newfound space: *What's underneath this urge?* That's where we're going next as we learn to truly *explore* the inner landscape of your patterns.

What you've learned in this chapter:
- *One conscious breath can change the trajectory of conflict.*
- *Exhaling activates your parasympathetic nervous system (via the vagus nerve).*
- *The pause is not about delay; it's about returning to presence.*
- *Small physical shifts can help anchor you during emotional activation.*
- *Breathing is not passive; it's a doorway to intentional choice.*

Chapter 6: Explore – Find the Pattern

"The curious paradox is that when I accept myself just as I am, then I can change." –Carl Rogers

The moment you pause, the noise settles just enough for something quieter to emerge. It's not silence, exactly, but a subtle shift, an invitation. The instinct to react is still there, pulling like a tide, but now you're not getting swept away because you were able to pause. You now have a chance to ask: *What is this really about?*

This shift opens up the space where your Self-energy, with its inherent qualities of calm and curiosity, can begin to lead. This is the second step of the method: **Explore**.

It's where you turn inward to listen. The urge you just interrupted didn't come out of nowhere. It arose from something: fear, history, longing, pain. Beneath every reaction is a reason, and this is the part of the work that helps you find it.

When we're in conflict, it's easy to stay on the surface: *They said this, so I did that. They pushed, so I pulled away.* However, healing doesn't happen on the surface. It happens when we trace the signal back to its source, when we take a moment to inquire into what set us off:

Why did that tone make you bristle?

Why did that pause make you panic?

Why did you suddenly feel twelve years old again?

These questions aren't meant to pull you into the past, but to loosen the grip it has on your present. They are to help you see that what feels overwhelming now might not be about this moment at all.

These kinds of questions help you peel back the layers, gently and honestly, so you can start responding from your truth.

We'll explore how to examine your reactions without spiraling into analysis or shame. We'll talk about how the nervous system encodes meaning, how to listen for what your body's trying to say, and how to begin rewriting the assumptions that shape your conflict story. The better you understand the alarm, the more you can respond to the situation rather than the story you're telling yourself about it.

☐ Ask yourself: What's the reaction you tend to judge most in yourself? What if, instead of fighting it, you got curious about the alarm it's trying to address?

Beneath the Urge: Listening to the Alarm

By the time you feel the urge to fix, flee, or retaliate, your nervous system has already decided: *This is not safe.* It's reading the situation through a complex filter of memory and pain, sending you urgent marching orders to shut down, make it better, disappear, or defend.

When you pause, you interrupt the reflex. Now, in that pause, you have a chance to *listen* to the alarm instead of obeying it.

That's what this step—**Explore**—focuses on. This is not about digging through your childhood in the middle of a heated moment. It's much simpler than that. It's asking, *What is my system trying to protect right now?*

Sometimes the fastest way to learn the answer to this question is through the body. Somatic therapists such as Peter Levine remind us that the body speaks the language of sensation. You may not know why you are reacting, but you can feel the tightness in your chest, the heat in your face, or the urge to get up and walk away. That's the alarm, and instead of numbing it or overriding it, this step invites you to notice it just long enough to decode the message underneath. For years, whenever I felt criticized, I would get a hot, prickly sensation across my shoulders and the back of my neck. I always thought it was anger. When I finally paused to explore it, I realized it wasn't just anger but the physical memory of bracing for impact, a feeling I traced back to a childhood where I learned to expect blame. The heat was my armor going up.

Other times, the entry point is a question. Byron Katie's work has been foundational here: When you find yourself caught in a story—*They don't respect me, I'm not good enough, I always mess this up*—you can gently ask, *Is that true?* Not to disprove it, but to loosen your grip on it just enough to breathe again.

You don't need to get to the root of the trauma right now and figure it all out. You just need to slow down the loop long enough to wonder *What else could be true?* Then *What do I need right now?*

Perhaps what you need is reassurance, a boundary, or simply the permission to walk away and speak the thing you've never let yourself say out loud.

When you give yourself that moment of honest inquiry, whether through sensation or language, you shift the entire trajectory of the conversation. You stop reacting from a version of you that's simply trying to survive and start responding from a place that's trying to connect.

The Stories We Inherit, the Stories We Carry

When you begin to explore what's underneath the urge, you'll almost always find a story, whether it announces itself as a flood of thoughts or just hovers in the background like emotional wallpaper. Sometimes the story is easy to name: *I always get it wrong. They're going to leave. I have to fix this.* Other times, it shows up more subtly: a tightening in your chest, a heat rising in your face, a familiar hollowing in your gut before you can even put words to what you feel. The story may not speak in complete sentences, but your body remembers every line.

That's the thing about these inner narratives: They rarely begin with us. They're handed down, absorbed, and inherited through what we heard, witnessed, felt, and sensed in the rooms we grew up in. Over time, we stop questioning them. We begin to wear them in our posture, our breath, our digestion, and our nervous system.

If you learned early that your emotions made others uncomfortable, your body may now react to conflict with constriction: a tight jaw, shallow breath, and muscles braced for rejection. If you were rewarded for staying quiet and agreeable, your nervous system may have paired compliance with safety, creating a legacy of tension in your shoulders or chronic fatigue that mimics shutdown.

This is not just metaphorical. As Peter Levine writes: *Trauma is not what happens to us, but what we hold inside in the absence of an empathetic witness.* What we hold inside often lives in the body long before it makes its way to the mind.

Neuroscience gives us more language for this. Your brain, especially under stress, does not passively observe the world; it predicts it based on what it has seen before. As Lisa Feldman Barrett explains in *How Emotions Are Made*, your brain constructs each experience in real time, using past data to guess what's happening now. So if your history tells you that anger leads to abandonment, your body might preemptively flinch at a raised voice even if this time is different. You aren't reacting to this moment. You are responding to the memory that resembles it.

You may not even know what story your body is carrying until it hijacks your breath or your voice mid-conversation. Ask questions like *Whose voice is this?* or *Where did I learn this rule?* It can feel disorienting at first—you're confronting the internalized strategies that kept you safe when you didn't have better options.

One of my clients (let's call her Anjali) always described herself as someone who "handled things well under pressure." However, in session, her hands were often clenched, her smile was tight, and her shoulders were drawn up around her ears. She'd talk calmly about conflicts with her partner, but the rest of her body was telling a very different story. It took time to realize that her steady tone was not coming from a grounded perspective. It was coming from a *freeze* perspective. The response came from decades of believing that anger meant danger, and that being nice was the safest way to keep love. When she finally let herself feel the heat behind her restraint, she wept from relief. She was not broken. She was rehearsed.

❍Ask yourself: When you find yourself pulling back, tensing up, or over-accommodating in conflict, what story might your body be holding? What does that sensation remind you of? Whose rules are you still trying to follow?

The goal is not to eliminate these stories overnight. They are part of your history, but they don't define your future. This step is about recognizing the script before it runs the show. It is about noticing the physical echo of an old belief and asking yourself, *Is this mine to carry now?*

For me, listening to what lies beneath the urge is one thing, doing it without getting lost in self-criticism is another. So I developed a structured practice for myself as a way to gently *find the pattern* without judgment. It became my compassionate investigation, and it always followed these three steps.

Find the Pattern

This practice helped me understand that the surge of panic, the urge to shut down, and the flood of anger didn't come out of nowhere. These responses came from a part of me that learned them long ago, often in situations where they were the only way to stay safe or stay connected.

This practice is about bringing compassionate attention to that part that steps in when conflict gets loud. The one that still believes you have to collapse to keep the peace or argue to stay in control. It's about seeing the strategy as a form of protection.

Here's how to do it:

Step 1: Spot the part

Who just showed up?

After the pause comes the noticing—not of what happened around you, but of what happened *inside* you as a part of you reacted. The reaction could be fast, loud, or so subtle you almost missed it, but it was there. This is the moment to notice not only that you got triggered, but *how*. Who took over the steering wheel? Was it the fixer? The avoider? The overexplainer? The person who smiles through clenched teeth and says, "It's fine"?

Perhaps it was a voice in your head whispering, *Don't mess this up*—or maybe it was a sudden need to retreat, lash out, or overperform. We all have these parts of our minds that are essentially ways of thinking, feeling, and behaving that make up our personality at any given time. These parts aren't flaws; they are brilliant adaptations that have kept us safe or at least functional. The challenge is that they tend to run on old scripts, reacting to the present moment with outdated rules.

Spotting the part is not about diagnosis or dissection. It's about gently acknowledging the shift in your internal system: *Oh. That part is here.* It might feel tight or buzzing. It might feel blank or rigid. You don't need a name for it, though sometimes giving it one helps. You can try something simple, like *the critic, the runner, the fixer, or the wall.* The part doesn't need to be perfect; it just needs to be *seen.*

Why it matters: When you recognize a reactive part as a part and not the whole of who you are, you create space for growth. You begin to *unblend* from it. Unblending is a core Internal Family Systems skill, and its goal is to differentiate parts from your Self. In IFS terms, this is the beginning of returning to Self: the calm, curious, compassionate awareness that can hold your reaction without becoming it. This shift is what makes it possible to respond from choice instead of automation.

Step 2: Ask what it's protecting

What is this part trying to prevent?
What happens if it does not jump in?
Once you've spotted the part that took over, whether it's a manager, a firefighter, or another protective part, the next step is to get curious about its role. This step is asking what this part, with its unique strategy, is truly trying to prevent. For instance, a manager part might be trying to avoid embarrassment by making you overexplain, or a firefighter part might jump in with anger to prevent you from feeling vulnerable.

Parts don't show up randomly. They are here for a reason, even if that reason no longer makes sense in your adult life. Some protect you from shame. Others are there to protect you from conflict, rejection, disappointment, or the terrifying feeling of being out of control. These parts learned that certain emotions, yours or someone else's, were dangerous—and they figured out how to keep things manageable.

So now, in the heat of a difficult moment, that part steps in without asking. It jumps into action, often with the best of intentions. The problem is that it often operates based on outdated logic. It's working off an old map.

This step is not about judging the part or rushing to fix it. It's about asking with genuine curiosity: *What is this part trying to prevent?* Or even: *What does it believe would happen if it didn't do its job?*

You might not get a complete answer. However, even a partial response—*It's trying to avoid embarrassment* or *It does not want me to get yelled at* or *It's trying to make sure I don't feel stupid again*—can soften something inside you.

Why it matters: Every reactive part is trying to protect something vulnerable. When you ask what it's trying to prevent, you begin to see that even the parts that frustrate you are acting out of care. That does not mean they should be in charge, nor does it mean they should be banished. Rather than allow the part to respond with its automatic charge, allow yourself to respond with curiosity and compassion—qualities of your Self that put you in charge instead of letting reactivity run the show. Curiosity disarms reactivity. Compassion gives you access to something bigger than your patterns: your ability to lead yourself. The IFS model asserts that the Self—the part that can help you lead yourself—is the essence of your being, possessing these eight qualities: compassion, curiosity, calm, confidence, courage, connectedness, creativity, and clarity.

Step 3: Notice the pattern

Where might I have learned this?
Can I respond from a different part?

Now that you've spotted the part and listened to what it's trying to protect, it's time to trace the pattern back to where it began—and forward to who you are now.

You don't need to revisit every moment of your childhood or recover the exact origin of your reactivity. You only need to sense the flavor of the story. When did this pattern start to form? When did you first learn that pleasing meant safety, freezing meant protection, or anger was the only shield?

Sometimes the memory is vivid: a parent's disappointment, a slammed door, a moment of humiliation in a classroom. Sometimes it's vague, more of a felt sense than a clear picture. Either way, what matters is not recreating the past but recognizing that it's showing up in the present. Once you see the pattern, you gain the power to respond differently. You can start unblending your Self from that protective part.

This is the moment to pause and reconnect with something deeper—a wiser presence inside you. The Self, the part of you that is calm, curious, clear, compassionate, and capable. You don't need to force that state. You just need to make space for it.

You might say silently:
Thank you for trying to protect me.
I can take over right now.
I've got this.
Sometimes a gentle statement is enough for the part to step back, and for you to step forward with more clarity and less urgency.

Why it matters: Tracing the pattern reveals that your reaction is not irrational; it's historical. Returning to Self is what keeps that history from defining who you are. When you can see the pattern and recognize the part with compassion, you loosen its grip. When you act from Self, you lead from the present, a powerful act of Self-leadership, grounded not in protection, but in pure presence. In IFS, the Self is considered the greatest healing force with a different resonance and energy than parts.

⟡Ask yourself: Think of a time recently when you responded in a way that didn't quite feel like you. What was the urge? What do you think it was trying to protect you from? What story or rule was your nervous system following? If you had taken just two minutes to explore what was underneath, what might you have noticed?

Start by pausing long enough to look underneath the urge. Your nervous system will still try to pull you toward what's familiar, and that's okay.

Now you have a way to gently interrupt the momentum, ask a better question, and move closer to a response that reflects your clarity rather than your history.

So much of what we call personality is actually a form of protection. It's not who we are, it's who we had to become. When you take the time to explore what's underneath the urge, you are unhooking from the script. You are turning toward yourself instead of abandoning what's true in favor of what's been practiced without reflection. This reveals your wisdom.

The more you do this, the more you start to see the gap—the space between what your nervous system wants to do and what your deeper Self knows is possible. From there, something else opens up: not merely insight, but choice.

We'll talk about what to do with that space—how to turn the pause and the insight into action, one that reflects who you are *becoming*, not who you've been trained to be. That's what this method ultimately asks of us: presence. A willingness to do something unfamiliar, freer, and that serves the moment, the relationship, and the Self.

The simplest way to start is to notice the move you usually make. Then imagine an alternative starting with the opposite: the one that feels outrageous, counterintuitive, even a little scary. For now, remember this: If your first move is the one you've always made, it might not be the only one available. You've cleared the ground, listened to the alarm, and identified the underlying patterns. Now it's time to choose a new path.

What you've learned in this chapter:

- *After the pause, explore what lies underneath the urge: fear, story, or protective parts.*
- *IFS helps you witness parts rather than obey them.*
- *Byron Katie's inquiry questions can soften the grip of your inner narratives.*
- *Your body holds clues; constriction, pressure, and collapse are data.*
- *"What else might be true?" is a powerful bridge to curiosity.*

Chapter 7: Engage – Flip the Script

You've made it through the first two gates. You noticed the pull—the urge to react, to fix, to disappear, to dominate—and you didn't let it carry you down that familiar reactive path. You explored what was underneath: the signal your body was sending, the story it was telling, the history it was echoing. That alone is huge. Most people never get that far.

This next part is where transformation lives. Even after gaining all that awareness and accessing your Self-energy in that space, you are still standing at a crossroads. The old paths are still right there. You know exactly how to walk them; you've done it a hundred times.

Now, there is a pause. A breath. A possibility. Inside that space, you get to ask, *What now?*

This is the moment to **Engage**. This is where the Exhale–Explore–Engage Method comes fully into view as a practice. The tool we'll use to access it is called *flip the script*. It's the moment of choice, the way we practice the Exhale–Explore–Engage Method in real time.

Engaging is about choosing *how* to act, *why* to act, and *from where* in yourself the action is coming. Are you reacting from fear or responding from a place of clarity? Are you trying to keep the peace or create it? Are you abandoning yourself or showing up for the relationship, including your relationship with yourself?

Sometimes engaging looks like setting a boundary. Sometimes it seems like staying open. Sometimes it's saying the thing you've been afraid to say, and sometimes it's choosing silence—but only if the silence honors you.

There is no formula here. The point is not to find the "right" answer—it's to find *your* answer, the one that reflects who you are when you are not being ruled by habit, legacy, or fear.

Many people get stuck here. They've paused, reflected, uncovered patterns, and then they freeze when it's time to act because what they *want* to do feels risky, like they are breaking some ancient rule they never agreed to but still feel bound by.

Remember, the discomfort of doing something new is not a sign you're wrong; it's a sign you're growing. There are also a few gentle ways to help you practice engaging with integrity, even when it feels scary.

Ask yourself: Can you remember a time when you almost said what you meant, honoring what you felt, but didn't? What stopped you? What would have changed if you had spoken your truth?

The Science of Choice

At first glance, it might seem like the Exhale–Explore–Engage Method is all about willpower: simply noticing your patterns and choosing differently. However beneath that simplicity lies something more profound. Choice—real choice—doesn't happen in a vacuum. It's shaped by biology, experience, emotional safety, and the stories we carry about who we are and what's possible for us.

We like to believe we're logical creatures making decisions through conscious reasoning, but neuroscience research—particularly the work around *predictive processing*—tells a different story. Your brain is constantly predicting what's about to happen, not merely waiting to react. It utilizes everything it has learned, from childhood experiences to yesterday's arguments, to create a mental model of the world and then fills in the gaps. It's like a GPS with your history hardwired into the route. So when something familiar happens—such as hearing a particular tone of voice, seeing a facial expression, or experiencing a sudden silence—your brain not only receives it, it finishes the story before the present moment has even played out.

Often, our options in conflict may feel automatic because we are not making decisions in real time. We're responding to what we *expect* to be true, based on the past. Our nervous system does not pause to ask, *Is this helpful?* or *Is this even real?* It simply executes the program that it has run a thousand times before. Those programmed responses once protected us, whether by creating safety, approval, or a sense of control, so they often feel not only familiar but *right*.

The default mode network, which we discussed earlier, plays a key role here. It's where we go to reflect, daydream, and reinforce our sense of Self. However, it does not distinguish between identity and adaptation. If your default mode network has internalized *I'm the one who stays calm* or *It's my job to smooth things over*, those legacy roles will shape your perception of what's possible even when they are no longer serving you.

Truly new choices can feel uncomfortable or wrong because the default mode network treats the familiar as safe, and the unfamiliar—even if it's more truthful—as risky.

That said, the brain is not a static entity. Through *neuroplasticity*, we know it's possible to change the default. We only have to disrupt the pattern long enough to install a new one. Techniques from somatic psychology, mindfulness, and behavioral science all rely on slowing down the process—widening the space between stimulus and response. That space, what Viktor Frankl famously called "our power to choose," is where the Exhale–Explore–Engage Method lives.

One surprisingly powerful way to expand that space is to imagine the *opposite* of what you are inclined to do. In creativity studies, this is known as *counterfactual thinking*: mentally exploring alternative outcomes that haven't yet occurred. It activates the parts of the brain involved in emotional regulation and creative problem-solving, helping you interrupt your autopilot and expand your response window. Adam Grant's research shows that people who engage in this kind of counterintuitive thinking are more adaptable, less reactive, and better able to regulate under pressure.

Let's say your instinct is to justify yourself, fix the problem, or apologize, even when it's not your fault. Before taking any action, pause and ask: *What would happen if I did the opposite? What if I said less? What if I didn't explain? What if I just stayed with the discomfort without trying to fix it?*

The moment you entertain that possibility, you open a door. Even seeing that the door exists changes your relationship to the room you're in.

This will also help you to *flip the script*, to disrupt your legacy response—not through sheer willpower, but by expanding your sense of what's possible. Before we go there, pause and consider this:

♡*Ask yourself: When was the last time you assumed your reaction was a conscious choice, but later realized it was just the best rehearsed option? If you could go back to that moment now, what's the most unexpected, opposite, or truer response you might have tried instead?*

That's the beginning of the Exhale–Explore–Engage Method: gently loosening your grip on the version of you that's been running the show through unquestioned patterns.

Flip the Script

By the time you've exhaled and explored, you've already done the hardest part: You've interrupted the autopilot and created space between the pull to react and the urge to disappear. Now, even though the familiar pattern might want to take the wheel—the part of you that knows how to survive by keeping the peace, proving a point, or shutting down—*you* have the wheel and don't have to hand it over.

For so long, this was the moment I would freeze. I could do all the breathing and reflection in the world, but when it came time to *act* differently, I'd fall back into my old patterns. I needed a final, decisive mental move—a way to interrupt my legacy script at the last possible second.

I started calling this *flipping the script*. It was more than a practice; it became my commitment to myself, a promise that I would no longer abandon my truth, even if my voice shook when I spoke it.

Here's how to do it:

Step 1: Name the move you are about to make
What response am I about to choose, and what's driving it?
By this point, you've already interrupted the cycle. You've felt the shift in your body. You've traced the pattern back to the part of you that took over, and you softened its grip on you. Now you are standing in a very different kind of space: the space where a choice is about to be made.

That choice might not feel like a choice yet. It might feel like momentum. You might still be stuck in familiar habits (to stay quiet, to defend, to take on the emotional labor of the room), but now, instead of reacting automatically, you pause and ask: *What response am I leaning toward right now? Does this feel like a conscious choice, or just the polished version of my old pattern?*

Perhaps you've done the work, but you're still tempted to explain, walk away, or offer a calm, well-worded boundary that's technically different from what you've said before, while still rooted in fear. That's okay.

This step is about naming what you are about to do and *noticing what's already in motion* as your first conscious option. You might realize it's still driven by a part that wants to avoid discomfort, or it might be a clearer move that still feels shaky or self-protective. Either way, naming it gives you the distance to ask, *Is this truly the response I want to lead with, or just a safer version of the same old strategy?*

Why it matters: This step helps you unblend from your protective patterns. It reengages your inner leader, what Internal Family Systems calls the Self, and places you in the seat of decision-making. You are flipping the script to honor who you truly are and to stop abandoning yourself in the moments that matter most.

Step 2: Flip it and expand it

What's the opposite of my usual move?

What else could I try?

Once you've named the response you're currently leaning toward, you're ready to expand your options. This is the moment to get playful, curious, and just a little bit braver because the response you reached for first might still be rooted in safety—not clarity.

Here's the invitation: *Try the opposite.*

But first, a crucial guardrail. The point of flipping the script is not to swing from one reactive extreme to another, especially if it leads to harm. If your default is to stay silent (a passive response), the opposite isn't to lash out with a verbal attack (an aggressive response).

Both come from a place of dysregulation. The goal is to find the *constructive opposite:* to move from a place of self-abandonment to self-honoring, or from protection to connection.

The true opposite of a harmful pattern is always one that fosters clarity and integrity.

⌒*Ask yourself: Does this "opposite choice" create more possibilities, or simply do more damage?*

Flipping the usual script helps interrupt your nervous system's assumption that there is only one safe way to respond. If your instinct is to explain, try staying silent. If your go-to is to smooth it over, try naming what's uncomfortable. If your default is to avoid, try staying a little longer. If your impulse is to hold it all together, try saying: "I'm not okay right now."

Then, add two more options. I practiced this for the first time with a friend who was consistently late.

My default was to say, "It's okay, no worries!" (appease).

The opposite was to say, "I'm upset that you're late" (confront).

But expanding the menu revealed a third option, the one that felt like a *body yes*: "Hey, I notice that when you're late, I feel a bit unimportant. Can we talk about that?"

It wasn't an attack or a surrender; it was just an honest statement.

Here are a few examples to get you started: You could say, "This does not sit right with me," and stop there. You could ask for a pause instead of powering through. You could write it down and come back when you feel clearer.

By looking at the opposite and the other possibilities, you are *widening the menu*. You are reminding your system that there is more than one way through this moment.

Why it matters: When your brain believes there is only one option, it perceives a threat even if that one option is polite or functional. Expanding your range of possible responses reduces reactivity and increases agency. This widens your window of tolerance, gives your system something new to practice, and lays the foundation for a different outcome.

Step 3: Try each one on

Which of these feels like a yes?

You've named the move you were about to make. You've explored a few other possibilities. Now comes the part that most of us were never taught how to do: Let your body help you make the decision.

This step is about resonance. Your choice shouldn't be based on what sounds best in theory, what would make you look good, or what would make the other person most comfortable. You are choosing the response that feels most aligned with your internal truth, even if it's unfamiliar, and even if it scares you a little.

To do that, you need to try each option on like a piece of clothing. Imagine yourself saying the words. Picture the moment of delivery. Feel the tone in your throat, the position of your shoulders, the expression on your face. Then ask the following questions: *Does my breath open or catch? Does my chest soften or harden? Do I feel grounded, or like I'm bracing defensively?*

When you turn inward, you are listening for a *body yes*—a subtle signal that says, *This feels more like me.* The problem for me was that for most of my life, I wasn't listening to my body. I had to learn my body's language—to distinguish between a full-body *yes* and that quiet, clenching *no*.

I stumbled upon the somatic work of Martha Beck, and it finally gave me a way to practice this. I started to think of it as my own body compass, and it became one of the most reliable tools I have. This is how I learned to use it.

How I learned to use my body compass:

1. **First, I had to learn to recognize my *yes*.** I would think of a time when I felt deeply aligned and authentic to myself. It didn't have to be a big moment, just one that felt right. Then I would close my eyes and scan my body, asking, *Where do I feel that* yes? *What is its texture? Its temperature?* For me, it was warmth and openness.

2. **Next, I had to find my *no*.** I'd then recall a time when I said "yes" when I meant "no," or stayed silent when I was screaming inside. I would notice how different that felt in my body. The "yes" was expansive. The "no" was a hard, tight contraction; it held its breath.

3. **Then I learned to use the compass in the moment.** Before making a choice in a conflict, I would imagine each option and

ask my body: *Which one feels more like that* yes? I began to trust that my truest clarity wasn't in my racing thoughts; it was in my breath, my spine, and the space behind my ribs.

◗ *Practice using your body's cues this week. Try it on low-stakes decisions. When a moment of conflict arises, remember: Your clarity may not come from your thoughts, but rather from your sensations.*

Why the body compass works

Your body is faster and wiser than your conscious mind. Long before you can explain what's happening, your nervous system has already made meaning through the process of neuroception. It constantly scans for safety, congruence, and alignment through sensation rather than logic. When something feels aligned, your body opens. When it feels wrong, your body contracts.

Your body may not always know what's right for everyone, but it knows what's true for you. It remembers what you needed, what you gave up, what you longed to say, and it knows when a choice reflects your integrity.

Listening to your body interrupts your default mode network and reengages your somatosensory pathways, allowing for new neural associations to form. In plain terms, when you feel the truth in your body, your brain can follow.

Why it matters Your nervous system is wired to respond before your mind makes sense of it. Letting your body help choose rewires safety into your decision-making process, making truth feel more familiar than fear.

Step 4: Choose the one that aligns
What feels like the truth?

This is the moment where the inner shift becomes an outer one, and you become ready to respond in a way that reflects who you are at this moment.

Choosing does not mean you'll feel totally confident. It often feels wobbly and exposed, as if you're standing at the edge of an old pattern and reaching for a new one without a guarantee of success. That vulnerability is the sign you are no longer merely surviving the moment; you are making the courageous choice to inhabit it.

Reflect on the options you tried. Which one felt like a *yes* in your body? Which one felt like it honored your values, even if it stretched your comfort zone? Which one reflects the version of you who wants to build trust, set boundaries, or speak from truth—not to control the outcome—but to stop abandoning yourself in the process?

This step is not about delivering a flawless response. It's about making the next move from a place of presence instead of protection.

That might sound like: *This is hard for me to say, but I want to try. I need a moment to gather my thoughts before I respond. I have been quiet, but that does not mean I agree. I'm not sure what happens next, but I don't want to go back to pretending.* You don't need to explain it. You just need to own it.

Why it matters: This step makes the internal work real. Choosing, even imperfectly, interrupts the loop of automatic behavior and lays a new neural track. It sends a powerful message to your nervous system: *You are safe enough to be honest here.* Even a small, shaky move toward alignment begins to retrain your system to associate truth with safety.

◯Think of a moment when you defaulted to your usual role. What were you trying to protect? If you had flipped the script, what three things could you have done instead? Which of them feels most like a yes in your body right now?

Next, we'll explore how to live that choice out loud. Choosing is one thing; following through is where change can really begin to take root.

Embody the Choice

By pausing, exploring, and flipping the script, you've found the response that feels truer than your impulse, kinder than your conditioning, and more grounded than either. This new response might be a sentence you've never said before, a silence that protects your peace rather than punishes, a new boundary, a gentler tone, or even a choice that surprises you. Then comes the hardest part: actually doing it.

We like to think that once a decision is made, the rest is just execution—but for many of us, especially those accustomed to people-pleasing, overfunctioning, or blending in, our bodies don't always cooperate with our newfound clarity. You might know what to say, yet your voice wavers or your hands get cold, while a part of you whispers that perhaps now isn't the right time, that you're being too much, and that it's simply safer to wait.

This is just a sign that your nervous system and your truth are out of sync. You've chosen something different, but your body still remembers all the times it was not safe to do so. Repatterning is already happening.

Embodying the choice is not only about saying the words or setting the boundary. It's about becoming the version of you who *knows* it's safe to do so. It's about letting your breath, tone, posture, and energy reflect the Self you are reclaiming—not the parts shaped by habit or fear. You are allowing the emergence of the Self-energy that exists underneath these habits.

Begin in the Body

Start small. Start with the breath. Because no matter how brave your choice is, your body has to carry it. Your nervous system will always ask, *Is this safe?*

Somatic practitioners like Peter Levine and Deb Dana have shown that microregulation, those tiny bodily signals we send ourselves, can be enough to help our system reorient in moments of discomfort. That means it's enough to offer your body cues that say, *I'm here. I'm okay. I can handle this.*

So before you speak or act, check in with your body.

Is your jaw clenched? Can you soften it?

Are your shoulders rising? Can you let them drop?

Can you feel your feet? Wiggle your toes.

Can you take one slow, steady breath with the exhale slightly longer than the inhale?

These are small things, but they make a big difference. They let your nervous system know: You are here, in a new moment, with new choices. You are not trapped in the past.

Let the Body Lead

When you are grounded, the words don't need to be perfect. What matters is that they come from a place of presence. You have to mean them. They must belong to *you.*

Say what you came to say, but say it from your whole Self. This might mean slowing down, letting silence do some of the work, or speaking in a tone that neither shrinks to avoid conflict nor puffs up to prove a point. It might mean saying one clear thing instead of a list of justifications. You don't need to explain your truth to make it acceptable. You only need to speak it with care and congruence.

One of my clients (let's call him Sam) used to feel intense shame any time he disappointed someone. He told me, "I'd rather take on more than tell someone 'No.'" The first time he was able to admit, "I don't have the capacity for that right now," he recalled that his hands were shaking. Afterward, however, he said something I'll never forget: "I felt my body rise to meet my words. That's never happened before."

That's the moment we're after. Not just *acting* from your truth, but *letting your body hold it with you.*

Stay With Yourself

Here's what no one talks about: Even when you say or do the thing that is aligned with your body and Self, a part of you might still feel like you're doing something wrong. That's normal.

Legacy conditioning doesn't disappear the moment we choose differently. Often, it gets louder. You set the boundary, and then the guilt creeps in. You speak your truth and then wonder if it was too much. You follow your compass, and your old programming says, *You're selfish. You're rude. You're making things harder than they need to be.*

This is the moment to stay with yourself, stay with the choice you made, and stay with the version of you who made it.

I often encourage clients to return to what we call the *balcony view*, a term from Ronald Heifetz's work on adaptive leadership.

When you're down on the stage, in the heat of conflict, it's easy to lose perspective. When you imagine yourself stepping back up to the balcony, you can reconnect with your *why*.

Why did you choose this path? What outcome are you trying to create? What would the future-you thank you for?

⟁Imagine a future version of yourself, five years ahead, who's been practicing this for a while. What would they say to you right now, in this moment of wobble? What would they remind you of? What do they know that you're just beginning to learn?

Hold the Embodiment After the Moment

Once the conversation ends, the embodiment continues because choosing differently can bring *aftershocks*. Your heart might race, you might want to send a follow-up text to smooth things over, you might question everything. That's not failure. That's just your system recalibrating.

It's important to allow space for this by taking a walk or drinking some water. You could try journaling about how you're feeling. Name the part of you that's scared and remind it who's driving now: the Self you are growing into.

Another client I worked with started adding a short mantra after hard conversations. She'd put her hand on her chest and say, "That was true. That was brave. I'm proud of myself." It might sound simple, even silly, but it anchored her in her choice and helped her body metabolize the shift.

The truth is, embodying this new way of responding happens not only through what you *do* in the moment, but also how you stay with yourself *afterward*. It's the difference between a fleeting performance and a lasting transformation.

So the next time you feel that familiar pull to go back to what's safe, what's known, what's always kept things smooth, keep in mind that you are learning how to *be* someone different, someone *whole*.

You've done the hard part. You've paused when it would have been easier to react. You've looked beneath the surface of your urge. You've traced the story not only in your mind, but in your body, and you *chose* something that reflects—not your fear or your conditioning—but your *truth*.

Then you lived it.

That's the core of this practice. Not only understanding how to choose differently, but doing it, moment by moment, conversation by conversation. That's how a new way of being is built: breath by breath, choice by choice, until what once felt unfamiliar starts to feel like home.

Even with this framework, life won't always follow a script. There will be messy moments, people who don't respond the way you hoped, situations that test your clarity—and sometimes you'll forget everything you've learned. That's part of the work, too.

But every time you flip the script, every time you respond in a way that honors your truth instead of your training, you are rewriting the story. You are proving to your nervous system that safety and authenticity can coexist.

That, more than anything, is what makes the Exhale–Explore–Engage Method so powerful.

Next, we're going to explore what it means to walk this path in relationships, parenting, work, and everyday life—not as a polished performance, but as an imperfect, ongoing practice.

You'll hear stories from others who've tried, stumbled, and found their footing again. You'll also be invited to consider: How might this look in your world, in your body, and in your voice?

The Exhale–Explore–Engage Method is not merely a framework. It's a way of living.

Now it's yours.

What you've learned in this chapter:
- *Choice lives in the space between insight and action.*
- *The Exhale–Explore–Engage Method is not always bold; it's congruent.*
- **Flip the script** *is the embodied practice of choosing differently.*
- *Your body compass helps identify which response feels most like a* yes.
- *Embodying the choice means speaking, pausing, or exiting with integrity.*

Chapter 8: When the Conflict Is Within You

There is a kind of conflict that no one sees, the kind that rages entirely inside you. On the surface, you might appear composed, capable, even cheerful, while a fierce battle unfolds beneath. It's a war between the part of you that yearns for change and the part that clings to certainty. It's a pull to follow the voice urging, *Go for it,* and the one muttering, *You're not ready.* The conflict may be between the part desperate for rest and the one refusing to stop hustling.

This is *internal conflict,* and for many of us, it's the most familiar kind. This type of conflict does not come with slammed doors or sharp words, but it can be just as loud and destabilizing. When no one else is involved, we rarely treat it like a real conflict. We just call it *being stuck,* or *overthinking,* or *beating myself up again.* But make no mistake: This is conflict, and it deserves to be understood.

I have seen inner conflict play out in various ways with my clients: the mother torn between building her career and feeling guilty for not being fully present with her kids; the leader who wants to delegate but believes that things won't get done unless they do it all; the client who dreams of leaving a relationship that depletes them but can't bear to hurt someone they still care about.

These aren't just hard decisions. They are emotional standoffs between different parts of you, each trying to protect something vital. Each "side" is trying to protect something important: safety, belonging, identity, purpose. And each side believes it has to win.

One of my most defining internal conflicts happened around the time I was leaving my corporate job. On paper, that job was perfect: the salary, the status, and the team I loved. Yet something inside me was shrinking. I felt like I was living a version of my life that may have checked all the boxes but was quietly draining my joy.

I kept telling myself it was just a phase, that I should be grateful, that I could fix it by switching teams or starting another side project. That's how my internal conflict played out: in endless justifications, in the tug-of-war between security and self-trust.

Looking back, I wasn't hearing just one voice; I was stuck between ten competing parts, each pulling me in a different direction—the voice of the Achiever, the Caretaker, the Inner Child afraid of being *too much*, the Practical Realist, the Rebel, the Perfectionist. They all had something to say, and none of them agreed, so I stayed stuck.

Until one day, I stopped trying to fix it and started getting curious about what each part of me was trying to protect.

That was when things began to shift. I learned to pause, to listen to the pull and the fear underneath it. Then, little by little, I began making choices that weren't about silencing one voice or obeying another, but about choosing what felt most aligned with who I was becoming.

⟡Ask yourself: What's one decision you've been turning over in your mind lately? Can you name the different "voices" or parts of yourself that have something to say about it? What is each part trying to protect?

Exhale: The Pull Inside You

Internal conflict doesn't usually arrive with alarms. Instead, it sneaks up slowly. A tightening in your chest when you think about making that change. A familiar ache in your jaw from clenching through one more decision you don't feel ready to make. It's quiet, but insistent, like a background hum you've learned to live with.

The impulse in these moments doesn't always look dramatic. It might even sound reasonable, responsible, or wise, appearing as *I just need to think this through a little more* or *I'll deal with it after things calm down.*

However, if you tune in more closely, you'll often find a deeper urgency: the relentless urge to solve it quickly, to make the discomfort disappear, to run, or to simply do what you've always done, even if it's the very thing keeping you stuck.

The first step is to notice the pull without judgment, but with presence. Notice the part of you that wants to act now, fix everything, please everyone, stay safe. That's the nervous system trying to restore balance in the only way it knows how. It makes sense. Uncertainty feels like danger when there is no one outside of you to blame or push against. So the tension builds, and the pressure to resolve it mounts. That need to resolve opposing beliefs is known as *cognitive dissonance*: the discomfort that arises when two truths feel incompatible but equally urgent.

In those moments, the most powerful thing you can do is to *breathe.* To interrupt the spiral of rumination, take a breath, even if it is for only one second. One full breath can disrupt the momentum of urgency. It's not about finding the answer, it's about creating enough space inside yourself to realize that you are not only demanding action—you are also listening.

That relentless internal hum was something I knew all too well; it felt like an engine I couldn't turn off. I learned that I couldn't outthink the anxiety, but I *could* ground myself in my body. Before I could even figure out what to *do* about a decision, I first had to practice just *being* with the conflict inside me. This simple check-in became my first and most essential move.

How I Learned to Feel the Shift in Inner Conflict

1. **I would sit quietly and ask myself, *Where do I feel this conflict in my body?*** I'd notice the pressure, the spinning, the hollow feeling, or the heat. My only job was to let it speak without trying to fix it.

2. **I would name the split.** I'd notice if one part of my body wanted to leap forward while another part froze in place. That feeling of being both urgent and paralyzed was an important signal.

3. **I would exhale.** That single breath became my pattern-breaker. It was my only chance to pause the internal argument before it accelerated into anxiety or frantic decision-making. I learned that all *I* had to do was notice that *I* was feeling pulled and then make the choice to stay with myself instead of rushing toward the nearest mental exit.

Sometimes that pause was incredibly uncomfortable. I'd feel the full weight of my indecision, caused by the tension between my conflicting parts, more clearly than ever. However, I came to see that this discomfort was a sign that I was in new territory: the place where choice resides. This was progress. The repatterning had begun.

Now when I notice that familiar sense of urgency creeping in, when I feel the need to fix, decide, or push through, I know I can pause for just ten seconds. I can take one deep breath.

Remember, the goal here is not to resolve the conflict; it's to stay with yourself long enough to notice what is happening inside you.

Explore: Listening to What's Underneath

Within Internal Family Systems, being conflicted is understood not as confusion but as complexity. You're not indecisive. You have different parts within you, each holding its own fears, hopes, and memories, all contributing to your internal emotional landscape. As discussed earlier, these include proactive manager parts that strive to keep everything orderly and safe by exhibiting controlling behaviors, such as perfectionism or overthinking. You also have reactive firefighter parts that rapidly deploy impulsive responses—like lashing out, numbing out, or self-sabotage—to douse existing emotional pain.

Behind the protective managers and firefighters hide the vulnerable *exiled parts*, which are often young and carry the heavy burdens of past trauma, overwhelming experiences, and neglect—and can manifest as pain, terror, shame, and despair.

When internal conflict arises, these different parts compete for dominance, creating tension within you. Perhaps one part yearns for change while another, often a Protector, is terrified of what that change might cost.

One part might insist on protecting you from making a mistake, while another is simply exhausted from constantly holding everything together. The goal here is not to silence any of them. It's to listen.

I did this once when deciding whether to make a big investment in my business. One part of me, the Practical Planner, was screaming about budgets and risk. Another part, the Visionary, was painting a picture of future success. Instead of letting them fight, I sat down and journaled a conversation between them.

The Planner said, *We can't afford a mistake right now*, and the Visionary replied, *But we can't afford to stay small*. Giving them both a voice didn't provide an immediate answer, but it lowered the panic and allowed me to see the valid point each was trying to make.

If the part of you that's yelling the loudest says, *You are going to ruin everything if you do this*, get curious.

☺Ask yourself: Who taught you that? When did you first hear it? What is this part trying to protect you from?

It's probably not the current situation that created that panic. More often than not, it's an old fear resurfacing in a new outfit—perhaps a *shadow aspect* of yourself that fears failure or a wounded inner child part that experienced deep disappointment.

Your job is not to figure out which part to listen to; it's to become the one who can witness all of them without fusing with any of them. Your role is the compassionate observer, the calm seat in the center of the storm.

☺It can be helpful to name the parts that you notice: the Doubter, the Perfectionist, the One Who Always Smiles. Let them speak. Just listen. Ask them, What are you afraid might happen if I act differently? What are you hoping to protect me from? What do you need me to hear, even if I disagree with you?

You might be surprised by what they have to say. The part that seems resistant might be exhausted. The one that's pushing for action might be terrified of being powerless again. The part that sounds harsh might still believe it's protecting a younger version of you that once felt small or invisible.

When you get quiet enough to listen, what initially felt like opposition begins to sound more like loyalty. These parts aren't trying to sabotage you. They are trying to keep you safe in the only way they know how.

When you find yourself caught in a tug-of-war between two options, there is usually an old story underneath each pull. One voice might say, *You can't risk that*, while another whispers, *If you don't, you'll regret it forever.*

These are not random thoughts. They are patterned responses. Each is rooted in some mix of memory, fear, and longing. The problem is not that they exist. It's that we usually believe them without realizing it.

Instead of trying to argue with yourself or force a decision, I invite you to slow down and ask: *Where did that thought come from?* You do not need to dig endlessly into the past; it is important only to notice the source. The tone. The emotional fingerprint.

⟳ *Ask yourself: Who does that voice sound like? When did I first start believing it? What is it trying to protect me from?*

Most importantly, ask, *Does it still serve me now?*

This is the heart of what I call compassionate investigation. You are gently examining what your mind is trying to do for you. Every story your brain clings to has a reason for being there, even the stories that are critical of you: those that blame and judge you. Those stories were learned, inherited, repeated, and rehearsed in moments when they made sense. Now they might be outdated or misaligned with who you are becoming.

Here are some questions I often use with clients, as well as myself, when I notice an internal signal:

What's the voice behind this story?

What am I afraid would happen if I didn't heed it?

What is this thought protecting me from feeling or doing?

Does this voice belong to me, or did I inherit it from someone else?

If I could speak from my wisest, most grounded Self, what would I say to this fear?

What else might be true that I haven't considered yet?

While this work starts in the mind, the body always has something to say. Sometimes you'll feel a clench in your gut or a hollow in your chest before your brain even catches the thought. These sensations are clues—a form of memory without words. The body remembers old moments of threat or rejection even when the mind has moved on. These bodily sensations often carry the imprint of our inner child's past experiences.

So take a moment. Scan your body gently.

Ask yourself: What does this part of me feel like in my body? Where is it holding tension, heat, or shutting down? What memory does it seem to be carrying? What would it say if I let it speak freely?

This is not about getting rid of anything. It's about making space for something new to take root. When the old pattern is recognized, its source is questioned, and the body's truth is acknowledged, something will begin to shift.

Learning about IFS and parts was a personal revelation, but for a while, it was still just a concept. To make it real, I had to learn how to engage in conversation with these conflicting parts of myself rather than letting them battle it out in my head. The *find the pattern* practice I'd used for external conflict became even more crucial for mapping my inner world when I found myself conflicted inside. Here are the steps for you to try:

Practice: Find the Pattern (During Inner Conflict)
Step 1: Spot the part
Who just showed up?
Is it the Inner Perfectionist? The one who pleases before they pause? The Protector who says, *Don't rock the boat*? Allow yourself just a little distance to see this part as a part, not the whole, of who you are.

Step 2: Ask what it's protecting
What is this part afraid will happen if I don't heed it?
Sometimes it's an attempt to protect you from feeling foolish, experiencing shame, or risking abandonment. Even if you disagree with its fear, for now, it's important to acknowledge it.

Step 3: Trace the pattern
When did I first learn this was the safe choice?
Can I respond from a different part of me now?
Let the memory, or the felt sense, surface gently. No need to dig.

Just listen. Once the part feels heard, invite your wise, grounded Self forward. It might sound like, *Thank you. I understand. I'll take it from here.*

⟢*Ask yourself: Pick one thought that's been looping in your mind about a current decision or conflict. What is this story protecting? Who taught it to me? Is there any part of me that knows a different truth?*

This step is not about changing your mind. It's about moving beneath the surface of your thoughts to the place where all your parts can be heard, and you, the whole you or Self, get to choose what comes next.

Engage: Choosing from Truth

By now, you've begun to make space for what's inside. You've paused, maybe only briefly, but long enough to notice the tug-of-war playing out in your mind. You've felt the urgency, explored the stories, and acknowledged the protectors doing their best to keep you safe. That pause has created something really powerful: *the possibility of choice.*

This is where you begin to engage with internal conflict—not as something to solve or silence—but as a space where you can step in differently with more honesty, more spaciousness, more alignment.

By noticing the parts that have been activated, you're not just reacting. You're mediating. By embodying this Self-energy, the calm, compassionate part of the system, you can listen to all the others, name what's happening, and make a grounded choice. The Exhale–Explore–Engage Method is not about choosing one part over another. It's about creating enough room inside yourself to hold the tension with care, understand what each part wants, and help find a better way forward.

Often, these parts carry roles that were assigned long ago: They may be there to avoid conflict, to keep the peace, to speak up before anyone else can hurt you, to hide your needs to avoid being a burden. Their loyalty is fierce, but their strategies are often outdated. The **Engage** step involves listening to each part's concerns and helping it evolve. A Protector who used to scream might learn to speak calmly. A part that used to disappear might learn to take up space.

Carl Jung's shadow work can be helpful here. We don't integrate by force. We integrate by negotiation. We give each part a voice and let the most grounded one lead. The key to finding peace when we feel conflicted is to flip the script *within ourselves*.

For me, just listening to all my parts was a huge step, but it wasn't the final one. Since I was the only one who could sit in the leader's chair and make a choice, I had to learn to consciously choose a path that honored my truth instead of simply allowing the loudest or most fearful voice in my head to decide.

Flip the Script: Navigating Inner Conflict

We've learned that when the conflict is internal, the struggle is not with someone else; it's between the parts of you trying to protect, please, perform, or stay invisible.

Your role is to create space for each one, to hear them out, and to understand what they want for you. Ultimately, all of our parts are trying to help us in some way, even if it does not seem like it.

Here's how you can use the *flip the script* practice with internal conflict:

Step 1: Name the default

What is the old pattern?

How do I normally respond in similar situations?

Instead of jumping into action or trying to make the discomfort go away, recognize the story and your default pattern.

Step 2: Flip the script

How can I respond in a way that honors my needs, but from a place of clarity?

Now that you understand your default, explore new options. What would the opposite response look like? What about other options you haven't tried before?

Connect with the Self, and let it lead this process. As you explore the opposites, remember the crucial guardrail we discussed: The goal is to find a *constructive* opposite—one that moves you toward clarity and connection.

Step 3: Try it on

Which responses create the most openness in my body?

Take a moment. Imagine living each option. Say the words in your head. Feel what happens.

Does your breath open or catch?

Do your shoulders drop or tighten?

Do you feel a flicker of relief, a sense of alignment, or truth?

The options that feel most like a *body yes*—the quiet voice of truth rather than urgency—are the ones to follow.

Step 4: Choose the one that aligns

What's one small step I can take that honors all of me?

The goal is to find a choice, an action, a response that reflects inner leadership, such as a sentence, a pause, a boundary, a hand over your heart, or a decision made with both courage and compassion.

One of my inner struggles was a years-long conflict between my inner Achiever and my inner Truth-Teller. The part of myself that sought recognition and certainty clashed with the part that yearned for purpose and freedom. I used to let the Achiever win until I started listening more carefully. What I heard, over and over, was not that either one was wrong but that both wanted to be part of the conversation. When I started leading from a place of Self and wholeness, I was able to give space to both—and that's when everything changed.

⟁Ask yourself: Think of a decision you've been stuck on lately. What's the usual script you follow when these situations arise? What's the opposite of that script? What's one small, grounded alternative? Is there something quiet, clear, and true that you haven't tried yet?

One of the most powerful aspects of this work is what happens when a client learns to recognize the conflict within and remains present with it long enough to choose differently.

Take Elena, for example. She came to a session overwhelmed by relentless harassment from her ex-partner, feeling trapped by the need to constantly monitor messages and dreading face-to-face interactions. On the surface, it seemed like an external conflict, but beneath it raged a profound internal one. A scared inner-child part, fearing retaliation and aggravation, insisted that she "had to" tolerate these interactions. This part's old coping mechanism was trying to manage her ex's emotional state to prevent further harm, creating a form of cognitive dissonance in which her actions (enduring harassment) conflicted with her deeper desire for safety and peace.

As we explored this internal tension, Elena connected with her Self, who could finally grant permission to set boundaries and ensure safety. This shift led to a profound realization: *she no longer needed to endure abuse out of a misplaced obligation* to stem her old fears.

Although initially embarrassed about enduring past abuse, she was also able to embrace the fact that her previous lack of awareness about her power had made earlier intervention impossible. Now, equipped with reclaimed agency, she chose to implement immediate practical measures, which included pursuing a restraining order while moving decisively towards safety and self-protection. This act of reclaiming her power from a place of strength was one of the most courageous things I have ever seen.

Remember Jason, who had always stayed "rational" in conflict? His internal battle was between the part of him that wanted to express his frustration with his partner and the part that said, "*If you speak up, you'll destroy the connection.*" He had always believed that neutrality was a strength until he recognized that it was his freeze response. After weeks of practicing the pause, in one session, he sent a short, honest message to his partner: "I want to stay connected, but I also need to tell you something hard for me to say." He thought it might cause distance, but it sparked one of the most open conversations of their relationship.

These micromovements are how internal conflict begins to shift: not with a dramatic epiphany, but with one different choice, made in the moment when it mattered.

By now, you might feel exhausted. Conflict—especially the kind that rages inside—can leave you bone-deep weary. You've carried fears, decisions, and responsibilities on your shoulders for so long. You've held yourself together when things were falling apart. You may be wondering: after all this work, will I ever feel normal again? Will I ever feel... happy?

If no one has told you yet, let me: *You are not broken. You are becoming.* This is not the end of your story; it's the beginning of a new chapter—one where you are the main character of your life again. The conflicts, the patterns, the roles that once defined you are not your forever identity. Right now, it might feel like you've lost pieces of yourself in all the tension and turmoil. But what if it is simply the old container that kept you small, and your true essence is what is taking its place?

You will feel light again. One day, you'll laugh and realize it's no longer a polite smile but a genuine laugh. You'll wake up, and the first thought won't be about stress or what you did "wrong." You'll step into a room and fully occupy your space, without shrinking, without apology.

None of this means the journey will be perfect. Healing and growth aren't a straight line; they are a messy, beautiful spiral. Two steps forward, one step sideways—sometimes you'll fall flat on your face, then get right back up. That's okay. That's what progress looks like: it's clumsy and nonlinear, and *it's absolutely worth it.*

When you stay with yourself and keep choosing your truth, moment after moment, you will be more than okay. You'll be powerful. In fact, you already are.

Internal conflict doesn't resolve with one choice: It softens, changes, and reappears in new forms. Every time you meet it with curiosity instead of urgency, you change the story and begin to trust yourself. You build this trust by choosing what is most true for you.

The more compassion you cultivate when you experience inner conflict, the more skillfully you can navigate the disagreements that happen outside of you, with partners, family, friends, or coworkers.

Next, we are going to step into the complex world of family conflict. Here, the dynamics often feel uniquely charged, rooted in old loyalties and unspoken rules. We'll explore how the Exhale-Explore-Engage Method can help you respond—not from reactivity or inherited roles—but from a place of presence, truth, and genuine connection. Let's dive in.

What you've learned in this chapter:

- *Inner conflict is often between different parts trying to protect you.*
- *Understanding concepts like projection, cognitive dissonance, and using tools, such as IFS, shadow work, and inner child work, offers deeper insight into your internal battles.*
- *You can listen to all of the parts with compassion.*
- *The pause helps you avoid rushing into a knee-jerk response.*
- *Flip the script means asking: What have I never tried before?*
- *Alignment comes from small, honest actions, not perfect outcomes.*

Chapter 9: When It's Family

*"If you think you're enlightened, go spend a week
with your family." –Ram Dass*

Family gatherings are the original emotional Olympics, where you are simultaneously trying to win gold in "Most Improved Adult Child" while also expertly dodging your aunt's questions about your life choices.

There can be so much more to family conflict than just disagreements, especially when you have to navigate old loyalties, unspoken rules, and roles you didn't choose but learned to inhabit. No matter how much work you've done, how many boundaries you've built, or how many hours you've spent in therapy, family dynamics can still pull you back into old patterns that don't reflect who you are, but who you had to be.

Maybe the parent who doesn't hear you unless you raise your voice pulls you into either exploding or going silent. Maybe a sister who still treats you like the reckless one, even though you've been a responsible adult for years, pulls you back into old patterns. On the other hand, your grown child may withdraw completely, leaving you unsure whether to give them space or reach out again.

Conflict in families rarely lives in the words exchanged. It lives in what goes unsaid. In the inherited beliefs, the lingering resentments, the roles carved out decades ago that everyone keeps playing because that's what keeps the system intact.

In blended families, the situation can become even more complex. You may be trying to build trust with a stepchild who views you as an intruder, or perhaps you're trying to co-parent with an ex who still attempts to control the narrative. You may feel torn between your partner and your kids, trying to prove loyalty to both and ultimately feeling split in two. In these situations, conflict does not always explode; it sometimes simmers. It shows up in who gets to speak and who gets interrupted, who gets noticed, and who gets overlooked.

According to family systems theorists like Virginia Satir and Murray Bowen, these dynamics occur to maintain homeostasis. Every family has an internal balance it tries to maintain. When one person grows, sets a new boundary, or starts saying what used to be unspeakable, it threatens the whole system because their change exposes the dysfunction everyone else has been avoiding.

I have worked with families where the most "difficult" child, the one acting out, withdrawing, or struggling at school, turned out to be the one most sensitive to the emotional undercurrents that no one was talking about. Children often become the bearers of family conflict symptoms. They express the tension that the adults won't name. The chaos doesn't come from nowhere; it comes from unmet needs, unspoken grief, and resentment passed down like an heirloom.

In post-divorce families, this is especially common. A child becomes the emotional caretaker for a struggling parent. The hierarchy gets flipped. A teenager takes on the role of mediator or becomes the "problem" to distract from a silent war between adults. In those moments, it's not about right or wrong. It's about what has not been healed. Unless someone is willing to pause and ask what the system is trying to preserve, those patterns will keep repeating generation after generation.

I have experienced this in my own life. I have stayed calm because I was scared of what would happen if I spoke my truth. I have tried to explain myself to someone who was not listening, just replaying their version of the story, and walked away feeling even smaller than before.

Family conflict doesn't only challenge your boundaries; it challenges your sense of identity, because these are the people who shaped your nervous system, your self-concept, and your earliest ideas about love and belonging. When they don't see you, misunderstand you, or insist you play the role they are comfortable with, it can feel like erasure.

◯Ask yourself: What roles did you play in your family growing up? Who did you have to be to be safe, loved, or included? How much of that role still shows up when conflict arises today?

Exhale: The First Reaction in Family Conflict

Family conflict is rarely about what's happening now. It's about everything that came before, and that's why the emotional charge can feel so outsized. A comment from your mother lands like criticism because your body still remembers how impossible it felt to please her when you were growing up. Your teenage daughter storms off, and something in you flares up from all the times you were silenced as a teen, when you vowed to do things differently.

When tension rises, your nervous system does not see your sibling, child, or parent; it sees a familiar threat and acts quickly.

Your jaw might tighten, your voice gets clipped, and the old impulse to control takes over. In a different response, your heart races, your mind goes blank, and you suddenly agree to something you don't want to just to get the conversation over with. Or your chest sinks with shame, your shoulders curl inward, and that old internal voice whispers again: *I'm the problem.*

In these moments, your body is trying to protect you and is doing so based on a script that may have been written decades ago.

I have worked with parents who feel flooded with guilt the moment they say "no" to their kids because some part of them still believes love must be earned by being "good." I have coached adult children who go cold and defensive on the phone with their father, even though they swore they wouldn't. The moment his tone shifts, they're instantly 6 years old again, bracing to be blamed.

As we discussed, our nervous systems are trained to prioritize speed and survival, and stillness can feel like surrender, especially when old family scripts tell us not to upset the balance. However, a pause does not mean numbing out. It's not checking out or performing neutrality. It's a conscious breath that interrupts autopilot and lets you stay in the moment without getting swept up in it.

⃝Next time you feel that familiar surge in a family interaction, don't try to fix it yet. Just name what's happening. "My chest is tight." "I feel pressure to fix this." "I notice the urge to shut down." Then breathe. Inhale for four, exhale for six. Feel your feet. Let your body know you aren't back in that old story; you are here.

The power of this moment is not in what you say or do. It's in what you don't rush to say or do. It's the space you create inside yourself to not collapse into a younger version of you or a role you've outgrown.

For me, family conflict was the quickest way to lose touch with my body. My thoughts would race, but my physical reactions—my stomach dropping when my kids' grandparents brought up my parenting, my throat tightening when my sibling sighed in *that* specific way—were always faster. I learned that I couldn't *outthink* the dynamic. My first move couldn't be to explain or defend; it had to be to notice the shift in my own body. This became my nonnegotiable first step to staying grounded.

How I Learned to Feel the Shift in Family Conflict

Here's what I started to do in those tense family moments:

o **I'd place my hand gently on my chest or stomach**, wherever I felt the heat. I would just acknowledge it internally, asking myself, "*What's happening in my body right now?*"

- o **I'd anchor to one point of contact:** My feet on the floor, the texture of my sleeve. This simple act reminded me that I was in the present moment, not twenty years in the past.
- o **I would take one slow exhale.** Not to solve the dynamic, but just to stay with myself inside of it.

♡Ask yourself: What's your body's first signal that you are sliding into a family role you didn't choose? What would it feel like to catch it sooner, to stay with it?

Sometimes the biggest act of presence is not responding right away: Just breathe through the noise until you remember who you are and how far you've come.

Explore: What's Underneath the Role You Play?

In family conflict, the real tension is rarely about what's being said. It's about what's being rehearsed again and again, often across generations.

If you are a parent, a sibling, a caregiver, or part of a blended family, you've probably noticed this: a simple disagreement spirals faster than it should. A request feels like a demand. A shrug feels like defiance. A question sounds like an accusation. Underneath your reaction is something older than the moment.

Family conflict tends to reawaken roles you never consciously chose: the Peacekeeper, the Overfunctioner who held everything together, the One Who Had to Fight To Be Heard, or the One Who Simply Gave Up Trying. For years, you may have called this "keeping the peace" or "being the responsible one," when in reality, you were enacting a form of self-abandonment cleverly disguised as care. These roles can sneak into adulthood, and especially into parenting. Suddenly, you are responding not only to your child's behavior, but to an echo of how your parents responded to you.

In blended families, the pattern can be even more complex. A child might align with one parent and resist the step-parent because of unresolved grief or loyalty binds. In these cases, the child becomes a symptom of the unspoken tension between adults. What appears to be defiance or withdrawal may be an attempt to restore emotional balance to a system that feels unstable.

In these complex situations, pausing is not always enough. You also have to get curious about the underlying family system: *Who is playing what role? What emotions are being carried on behalf of someone else? What unspoken rules are shaping everyone's behavior?*

Here are a few questions that can help you start that exploration:

- *What role am I stepping into right now, Rescuer, Fixer, Rebel, Pleaser, Judge?*
- *When did I first learn this role? Who modeled it for me?*
- *Is this behavior mine, or am I carrying something that doesn't belong to me?*
- *What's the family belief or rule I'm bumping up against here? (e.g., "We don't talk about feelings," "Don't upset Mom," "You are the strong one.")*

o   *What does this dynamic want me to keep doing? What might happen if I don't?*

In IFS language, these are *legacy burdens*—ways of coping, protecting, and maintaining connections that were passed down, often unconsciously, from generation to generation. In high-stress moments, they speak loudly.

For me, this showed up as an obsessive need to clean everything up immediately after a family dinner, even when I was exhausted. It took me years to realize I wasn't just "being helpful." I was reenacting a role I learned from my grandmother, who believed not leaving a mess overnight was the best way to prove her worth as a hostess. My hands were washing dishes, but my nervous system was trying to secure my sense of belonging.

It's not enough to notice your emotional reaction. You also must track who or what is behind the wheel. In my case, sometimes what looked like "being a good parent" was a part of me playing out a role I learned decades ago.

For me, reading about family roles in a book was one thing, but seeing them play out at my holiday dinner table was another.

Knowing I was playing a role wasn't enough; I had to get specific in finding out, *What role is this? The Peacemaker? The Responsible One?*

To get clear, I started using the *find the pattern* practice specifically for these dynamics. Doing so was like turning a spotlight onto the stage of my family drama.

Here is the *find the pattern* practice if you'd like to try it:

Practice: Find the Pattern (in Family Dynamics)

Once you've paused and felt the shift, the next step is to get curious.

Step 1: Spot the part

Who just showed up?

Was it the Overfunctioning Oldest Sibling? The Peacemaker who learned to avoid conflict at all costs? The Teen who still braces for disapproval? Family conflict tends to activate parts of us that were forged early, and those parts show up fast.

Step 2: Ask what it's protecting

What is this part trying to prevent?

Perhaps it's an attempt to avoid rejection, shame, or the feeling of being misunderstood. These parts are trying to protect you even when their tactics feel outdated or exhausting.

Step 3: Trace the pattern

Where might I have learned this? Can I respond from a different part?

You don't need to dig deep into childhood to sense the legacy. Just ask, *Is this mine, or did I inherit it?* You might even silently tell the part, *I see you. I know you are trying to help. I've got this now.* This shift—tiny, internal, invisible—is the beginning of a new script, one that reflects the adult you are now, not the child you once were.

⏹*Ask yourself: What part of you shows up most often in family conflict? What is it trying to protect? What would it need to loosen its grip, even just a little?*

No need to fix the dynamic in one conversation. You only need to become aware of it. Then, from that awareness, you will be ready to respond with something new.

Engage: When You Are Ready to Respond Differently

Family conflict has a way of instantly making us forget who we are. One glance, one sigh, one sentence can instantly transport us back to being six years old, arguing over who left the door open or trying desperately not to upset someone who's already emotionally teetering. So, when it comes time to **Engage**, choosing a response that reflects your truth is not about finding the perfect words.

The Exhale–Explore–Engage Method does not ask you to be calm, composed, or even kind all the time. It asks you to *align* with your values, integrity, and the person you aspire to be. It will look different depending on the situation. Sometimes it means speaking up. Sometimes it means setting a boundary. Sometimes it means letting silence do the talking. Let's look at some examples.

Case Study: From Collapse to Clarity

Jason, whom you met earlier, was raised to be *the calm one*. In his family, emotional outbursts were met with either withdrawal or ridicule. So when his teenage son started slamming doors and challenging rules, Jason's habitual response was to say nothing, to weather the storm quietly and hope it would pass. Over time, however, that silence turned into resentment.

In one coaching session, we traced the legacy. For him, silence equaled safety. We also named the cost. Jason was teaching his son the same message he had once internalized: that anger breaks the connection, and no one wants to hear your feelings.

The next time a blow-up happened, Jason tried something different. After his son stormed off, Jason took five minutes alone. He breathed. He acknowledged the urge to collapse, and chose not to. When he reentered the room, he said, "I want to understand what's going on, but I can't do that when we're yelling. Let's try again when we're both ready."

That was it—just a moment of alignment. Jason didn't default to silence or explode to match his son's energy. He engaged in a different way from a grounded middle. His son, while still frustrated, didn't leave. He nodded. That was new.

Use the Birds-Eye View

When you're in the midst of a family pattern, the most helpful thing you can do is step back.

⟡Ask yourself: What kind of relationship do I want to build here? If I respond from autopilot, where will this likely go? What response, even if it's hard, moves us toward trust, clarity, or healing?

This works especially well with adult family members. When your mom makes a subtle dig about your parenting style, your brother blames you for a holiday schedule conflict, or your teen rolls their eyes and storms away, pause. Ask, *What outcome do I want? And what choice reflects that?*

Flip the Script: Practice for Rewriting Your Family Role

For me, seeing the pattern was liberating, but the real freedom came when I realized I didn't have to keep playing the part. As the adult in the room, I could choose a different line. This was the most challenging and most empowering part of the work—learning to *flip the script* at home to start being myself. Here's how to flip the script when you're caught in a family pattern:

Step 1: Name your default

What do I usually do in this situation?

Notice what part comes in: the Fixer, the Explainer, the Peacemaker, the Avoider, the One Who Folds First. These roles may have once kept the family system stable, but they often require you to disappear.

Step 2: Flip it, and expand it

What's the opposite of that move?

What else could I try that I have never practiced?

If you usually stay quiet, what would it mean to speak? If you usually explain, what would it mean to say, "I'm not available for that conversation right now"? Additional moves: "I hear you, and I also need to take care of myself here" or "Let's revisit this when we're both calmer."

When exploring the opposite move, hold onto the guardrail we set earlier. With family, this is critical: The aim is to find the *constructive opposite*. If your default is to absorb tension to keep the system stable, the opposite isn't to create an explosion; it's to introduce a response that brings clarity and connection without attacking.

Step 3: Try each one in your body

Say each option to yourself. Imagine delivering it, one at a time. Does your breath deepen or get stuck? Do you feel softer or like you are bracing? Are your muscles relaxing? Chest expanding? Or is it the opposite? Look for the *body yes*, the option that feels most like self-alignment, even if it's uncomfortable. That's the one to follow.

Step 4: Choose the one that aligns

Select the response that not only protects you but also represents you. Not the version of you the family trained you to be, but the one you're becoming by choice.

♡Ask yourself: Think of a family dynamic that feels stuck. What's your usual script? What would it feel like to try something new to practice freedom? What might shift if you did?

Case Study: Rewriting the Step-Parent Story

Elena, our co-parenting client from Chapter 5, would frequently default to overfunctioning during tense conversations with her ex. However, the pattern was not limited to him. In her blended family, she noticed herself bending over backwards to "earn" her stepdaughter's affection while never expressing when she felt disrespected or dismissed.

One day, after a particularly tough exchange, Elena paused. She named what she wanted (to feel respected and included) and realized that her usual strategy—pleasing and pretending—was not getting her there.

She tried something new: "I want us to have a good relationship, and I know I have avoided hard conversations, but I need to be honest with you about how that felt."

It was not easy. Her stepdaughter didn't apologize right away, but the energy shifted. It was the first time Elena didn't disappear to keep the peace. That act of alignment, choosing her truth over her pattern, became a turning point in how she showed up in both households.

Family brings out the oldest parts of us: the Child Who Wants to Be Chosen; the Teen Who Wants to Be Heard; the Adult Who Just Wants Peace and can't figure out why it always feels so fragile. These dynamics run deep because they were formed in the soil of our earliest belonging. We didn't choose the roles we inherited, but we continue to play them long after they stop serving us because they once helped us survive.

That's what the Exhale–Explore–Engage Method offers us

here—not a script to fix our families, but a path back to ourselves *inside* our families. It provides a way to notice when we're reacting from habit or the wounds of our lineage and gently make a different, consciously chosen move.

Truth does not always mean confrontation. Sometimes it means clarity, letting go of a dynamic that is not yours to fix, or showing up differently, even if no one else does, simply because *you* want to live in integrity with who you are becoming.

When we choose differently, when we pause, reflect, and act from a place of presence, we begin to reshape what's possible for everyone around us. Kids notice when the adults around them speak from a place of calmness. Siblings feel the shift when old competition gives way to compassion. Parents soften when their grown children show up with boundaries and love instead of blame.

You don't need your whole family to change for you to feel free. Reclaiming your freedom is about finding your voice within the story, recognizing when your body is about to walk the same old path, and offering it a new one.

♆Ask yourself: Who do you become in your family when things get hard? What would it look like to respond from the version of you who is no longer trying to prove, please, or protect, but simply trying to live from truth?

Next, we'll step into romantic partnerships, where the intimacy is different, the stakes often feel higher, and the old patterns don't stay hidden for long. The Exhale–Explore–Engage Method applies here too, and when it's chosen with care, it can change not only the conflict but the entire fabric of your connection.

Are you ready to dive into that conversation?

145

What you've learned in this chapter:

- o *Family roles are sticky and often invisible until they are challenged.*
- o *Pausing helps you respond as the adult you are now.*
- o *Flipping the script enables you to step out of your old role (e.g., Fixer, Ghost, Rebel).*
- o *Repair does not always require confrontation; sometimes it means quiet clarity.*
- o *You don't need the whole system to change for you to feel free.*

Chapter 10: Conflict with Your Partner

"The quality of our relationships determines the quality of our lives." –Esther Perel

Conflict in romantic relationships carries a different charge: You feel more exposed, more vulnerable, and the conflict is more entwined with your sense of worth and safety. With family, even when it's messy, there is often an invisible safety net—some part of us that assumes, no matter what, they are still *my parent, my sibling, still my child*. However, with romantic partners, that safety net often does not exist. Love feels conditional. Connection feels earned. When conflict arises, the entire relationship, and perhaps even your lovability, is on the line.

Romantic relationships don't merely expose your triggers. They amplify them. This is someone who sees you every day, who knows your stress signals, and who can trigger you with a sigh or silence. When you care, because there is intimacy and high stakes, your nervous system does not merely respond—it reacts. It panics.

While romantic relationships lack the explicit roles found in family dynamics—there aren't defined roles like "eldest daughter" or "baby brother"—the choices you make are still shaped by your earliest relationships, by what you saw modeled, what you learned to expect, and what you believe love should feel like. If conflict was loud or volatile in your childhood, you might shut down completely when your partner raises their voice. If love meant caretaking or self-sacrifice, you might give too much and resent it later. These aren't flaws. They are echoes, and they show up most vividly where you are most exposed: in love.

◯Think about a recent argument or tense moment with a partner (current or past). What did it bring up in you? Were you trying to win or to be heard? Were you protecting yourself or trying to preserve the relationship? What part of you was running the show?

Romantic conflict pulls on many threads: desire, trust, power, safety, and attachment. According to attachment theory, the patterns we formed with early caregivers continue to play out in adult relationships. Anxious types may seek reassurance mid-conflict and spiral when it's not offered. Avoidant types may retreat, shut down, or deflect. Disorganized attachment, often rooted in trauma, can swing between anxious pursuit and avoidant retreat. While these styles are adaptive, they also shape how we interpret conflict: Is it a rupture we can repair or a threat we must flee?

Internal Family Systems theory can be profoundly helpful here. As you've learned, conflict with a partner rarely stems from your whole Self. Instead, it often arises from a protective part stepping in when deeply held attachment needs for nurturing, protection, and wisdom remain unmet. For example, if your partner pulls away, it might activate a firefighter part in you that lashes out—or overpursues your partner, trying to force closeness or resolution—out of fear of abandonment. Conversely, a manager part might insist on emotional distance or excessive rationalization to prevent the vulnerability that intimate conflict often demands. That's often the reason couples get stuck in reactive loops. Protector parts clash while the exiled pain underneath stays unheard.

Let's examine how we can break these loops by reconnecting you with *your whole Self* within the conflict. Intimacy is not developed because we avoid hard conversations; it comes from staying connected through them—from choosing to speak, listen, or pause—not out of fear or old scripts, but from alignment with what's true and needed.

You'll meet two of my clients: Sophie, who stayed quiet to maintain peace, and Adam, who argued to feel in control. You'll hear how they began to recognize their patterns, trace the stories that drove them, and show up more consciously. You'll also see how, over time, this changed not only their fights but the fabric of their relationship.

So if you've ever walked away from an argument wondering, *Why did I say that? Why didn't I say more? Why does this feel so familiar?* This is for you.

When you stop reacting from pain and start responding from presence, something radical becomes possible—a deeper, safer connection.

Exhale: What Romantic Conflict Feels Like in the Body

If you've ever felt like you were suddenly five years old again during an argument with your partner, you're not alone. Romantic conflict can trigger our earliest emotional wiring faster than almost anything else. Even when we think we're staying "adult," our bodies often tell a different story.

You might feel your chest tighten when your partner criticizes something small or your jaw clench when they go quiet. You might suddenly need to fix the conversation, escape it, or prove that you are right. Perhaps your brain goes blank; you can't find words, and later, you'll play the whole conversation in your mind with brilliant clarity, wishing you'd said that one line, asked that one question, held your ground.

Those ineffectual responses are simply your nervous system following patterns it learned long ago.

For people with anxious attachment patterns, romantic conflict can feel like a life-or-death moment. Your partner pulling away, shutting down, or delaying a response can activate a deep fear of abandonment. You might frantically text, push, overexplain, cry, or beg—for closeness, for repair, or for relief.

For those with more avoidant strategies, the same conflict might make you feel cornered. You might disconnect or try to shut it down fast because your system interprets emotional intensity as danger. Conflict does not feel like an opportunity; it feels like a trap.

If your history includes unpredictable or unsafe caregivers, you might bounce between the two. One moment, you are desperate to connect; the next, you are desperate to get out.

Nowhere did my body speak louder or faster than in my romantic relationships. One wrong look from my partner, one particular sigh, and I could feel my whole system go on high alert. My brain would go blank. I learned that before I could even *think* about what to say, I had to find my way back into my body. This simple check-in wasn't just a tool; it became a lifesaver for me.

How I Learned to Feel the Shift with My Partner

When I felt that flash of heat or the clench in my gut, here's what I practiced:

1. **The first thing I would do is touch my own body.** I'd place a hand on my chest or stomach and just say internally, I feel it here. *I'm here.*

2. **Or I'd press my feet into the ground.** This simple act reminded my nervous system that I was physically safe, even if my emotions were in a storm.

3. **I would take one slow exhale.** Not to fix my partner or the situation, but just to stay in the moment with myself.

⟁In your next argument or tense moment, ask yourself: What's your body's first cue that you're leaving yourself? What would it feel like to stay in contact for one breath longer than usual?

The pause is where your power lives, but it's also the hardest thing to reach in the heat of the moment. That's why, in romantic conflict especially, the breath matters. The long exhale, the dropped shoulders, the three seconds where you resist the urge to fill the silence, to interrupt, to make the discomfort go away.

Somatic therapist Resmaa Menakem talks about *clean pain* and *dirty pain*. Clean pain is the discomfort that comes with growth: being honest, being vulnerable, staying present. Dirty pain is the pain we create when we avoid clean pain. When we blow up or shut down, when we say "yes" to avoid a fight or withhold to make a point, that's dirty pain. The pause invites us into clean pain. It's rarely comfortable, but it *is* clarifying.

Even one deep breath can interrupt a cycle, making space to notice which part of you is reacting and deciding if that part needs to be in charge right now.

○*In the next heated moment with your partner, see if you can catch the first impulse and breathe through it instead of acting on it. What becomes possible when you don't rush to respond?*

Explore: What's Really Going on Beneath Romantic Conflict?

It's easy to think the conflict is about what's being said: the dishes, the phone call that was not returned, the difference in parenting styles. However, underneath the words, something more profound is almost always unfolding: a story about safety, about worth, about love. It's usually *not about this moment*; it's about every moment that came before it. In IFS terms, the part of you that reacts in conflict is not *you*, it's a protector. This part learned to step in fast when something felt threatening. Perhaps it's the one that tries to fix things, becomes sarcastic, or shuts down and disappears altogether. These parts aren't trying to sabotage your relationship; they are trying to protect you.

The deeper work in this **Explore** stage is to bring your Self-energy to these protective parts, understanding that they often carry old narratives and fears from long before your partner even arrived.

For example, if you grew up in a home where expressing needs led to punishment or rejection, then asking for something in your relationship might feel excruciating. Even a kind, simple request could activate the old belief: *If I say what I need, I'll lose love.* So the conflict ensues—not only between you and your partner, but also internally between the part of you that wants closeness and the one that's terrified of what it might cost.

⟲*When you find yourself in conflict with a partner, ask yourself: "What am I making this mean?" Is it really about what's being said, or is your system responding to a deeper fear of not being seen, not being safe, not being enough?*

The work of unpacking old stories starts here. Your mind might say, *He's ignoring me,* but the deeper story might be that *people always leave me,* or *she never listens,* when the real wound is *my voice has never mattered.* My version of this used to surface whenever my partner needed space after a tense moment. His quietness was just a request for a pause, but my nervous system translated it into the ultimate rejection. My internal story wasn't *he needs a minute*; it was the old, terrified whisper from childhood: *I am too much, and now I'll be abandoned.* It took practice to learn to offer him space without my fear overtaking me in that silence.

Practice: Find the Pattern (in Romantic Dynamics)

Once you've paused and felt the shift, the next step is to listen to the part of you that became activated. Underneath the raised voice or polite silence, there is often a younger version of you trying to stay safe.

Step 1: Spot the part

Who just showed up?

Is it the Fixer who can't rest until harmony is restored? Is it the pleaser who says "yes" even when you mean "no"? Is it the Protector who needs to win the fight so you don't lose the relationship?

Step 2: Ask what it's protecting

What is this part afraid might happen if I don't heed it?

Often, these parts are trying to avoid abandonment, failure, rejection, or humiliation. Even if their methods aren't working, their motives are rooted in care.

Step 3: Trace the pattern and return to Self

Where did I learn this strategy?

Then, silently or aloud, you could let that part know, *I see you. I know you are trying to help. But I have got this now.*

When you lead from Self rather than from a wounded part, you create enough space to see your partner not as the enemy, but as another person with their own parts, patterns of behavior, fears, and longing for repair.

♡*Ask yourself: What version of you tends to show up in conflict with your partner? What's it trying to protect? What would change if that part didn't have to carry the whole conversation (or shut it down)?*

Another client of mine, Emma, used to downplay her needs in relationships. When her partner forgot a special date or dismissed her feelings, she'd smile and say, "It's fine." However, inside, she'd feel hollow. During one session, she realized that "it's fine" was her Protector's way of avoiding rejection. That part had learned that being easy to love meant being easy to please. Once she saw it for what it was—a loyal but outdated strategy—she began experimenting with honesty in small, brave moments. "That hurt," she practiced saying. "Can I tell you why this matters to me?"

Exploring is not about blaming yourself or your past. It's about gently loosening the grip of the old map so you can start drawing a new one—one where your truth and connection don't have to be at odds. One where your voice belongs, even in hard conversations.

Engage: Choosing a New Response in Romantic Conflict
The moment between recognizing the pattern and choosing something different is where the Exhale-Explore-Engage Method

comes alive. In romantic relationships, that space holds both tenderness and power. The goal is not to win the fight or erase the tension; it's to maintain integrity while creating space for a genuine connection.

Engaging from the Exhale–Explore–Engage Method does not mean you suddenly become flawless at communication. It means you become *more* honest with yourself. You stop responding from the scared part, the appeasing part, the shut-down part, and begin to let your values steer the conversation.

♡Ask yourself: What outcome do I want in this moment? Not what would avoid discomfort or keep the peace, but what would bring you closer to truth, intimacy, or repair?

This is the moment for visiting *the balcony*, zooming out to see what matters most. When you're lost in the emotional weeds, it's hard to remember that you are shaping the future of your relationship.

Case Study: Jason's Freeze

Let's return to Jason, the client who prided himself on being the calm one. After doing the work of *Exhale* and *Explore*, he realized his "calm" was actually a freeze. When conflict arose, he would retreat into silence and compliance, then later withdraw emotionally or become sarcastic.

During one particularly tense conversation about finances, Jason noticed the urge to shut down, but instead of defaulting to silence, he said, "I want to keep talking, but I can feel myself freezing. Can we take a fifteen-minute break so I can come back to this with a clear head?" It was awkward, imperfect, and yet completely transformative. His partner felt respected instead of stonewalled—and Jason, for the first time, felt a deep sense of pride in how he'd both stayed in the conversation and stayed true to himself.

Case Study: Emma's Apology Pattern

Emma had a deeply ingrained habit of apologizing in the heat of conflict because she'd learned that apologies calmed the storm. After naming this legacy pattern, she tried something new. The next time her partner criticized how she handled a scheduling mix-up, instead of apologizing reflexively, she paused and said, "I hear that this was frustrating for you. I'd like to walk through what happened before we decide what needs to change." That moment was a turning point—not only because the conversation went better, but because *she* felt more grounded in how she showed up. She was learning to dismantle a lifetime of self-abandonment cleverly disguised as care, one conversation at a time.

Choose From the Balcony

When I was lost in the emotional weeds of an argument, it felt impossible to remember what really mattered. I could feel like I was fighting for my life over who was right about the dishes. I came across an idea from negotiation expert William Ury about *going to the balcony*, and I adapted it for myself. It became my emergency exit from the drama. In the middle of a fight, I would imagine myself floating up to a balcony overlooking the room. From that distance, I could see both of us more clearly. Up there, I would ask myself the only questions that mattered:

What truly matters to me in this relationship beyond this fight?

What kind of connection am I trying to build in the long run?

What response, right now, moves me closer to that vision?

Seeing my patterns and taking the balcony view was half the battle. The other half was *choosing* a different response in the heat of the moment. For years, I felt like my only options were to fawn, defend, or shut down. Learning to *flip the script* in my relationship meant choosing my integrity over my old habits, even when it felt terrifying. Here is how you might try it:

Flip the Script: Rewriting Your Role in Romantic Conflict
Step 1: Name your default

What do I usually do when tension rises with someone I love?

Do you fawn? Defend? Numb out? Overexplain? Pretend it does not hurt? Name your urge to bring it into the light. Awareness is how you begin to loosen the grip.

Step 2: Flip it, and expand it

What would the opposite look like?

What are two other things I could try?

If you usually explain, try naming just one feeling. If you usually say, "It's fine," try "It's not fine, and I'd like to talk about it." If you usually shut down, try "Can we pause? I want to stay present." Now add two more options, ones you've never practiced, but that might create space: "I'm struggling to say this clearly, but I want to try" or "I care about us. I also need this to feel mutual."

As you explore the opposite, remember the guardrail from Chapter 7. In the intimacy of a partnership, where you are most exposed, the goal is the constructive opposite. If your pattern is to make yourself smaller to keep the peace, the opposite isn't to launch a blame-filled attack. It's about finding a response that invites genuine connection rather than creating more distance.

Step 3: Try each option in your body

Once you've imagined three possible responses, check in with your body. Say each one silently, and feel what happens. Do your shoulders soften? Does your breath deepen? Do you feel a flicker of alignment? That flicker is your *body yes*.

Step 4: Choose the one that aligns

Pick the response that reflects who you want to be in this relationship—not who you had to be in the last one. It's okay if that response feels wobbly in your voice but solid in your gut. Flipping the script in love means you no longer prioritize comfort over truth or connection over self-respect.

❍*Think of a recent conflict with your partner and ask yourself: What did you default to? What were you protecting? What would it feel like to choose from your clarity and courage?*

The truth is, the people we love most are often the ones who trigger us the most, as they bring us face-to-face with our hopes, our fears, and every legacy we've inherited about what intimacy should look like.

If you've ever walked away from a conversation with your partner and thought, *That was not me*, you know how painful it can feel to show up from your outdated patterns instead of your truth. However, you also know the longing underneath it: the desire to be seen and to stay connected without disappearing in the process.

That's what the Exhale–Explore–Engage Method makes possible: honest repair and deep trust, the kind that emerges when you're willing to bring your whole Self to the relationship, especially when it gets messy.

You'll still get it wrong sometimes, and so will they. What changes is that you'll know how to pause, how to listen to your urge without obeying it; how to hear your legacy pattern whispering and gently set it down.

You'll know how to ask: *What actually matters here?* And more often than not, you'll be able to choose accordingly.

That's how love grows. It's not always about getting it right, but rather about returning to yourself and each other, again and again.

⟲*When was the last time you had a conflict with someone you love and left the conversation feeling more connected than when it began? What helped that happen? What made it feel safe to be honest?*

Next, let's explore conflict with people who are not your family or your partner—your friends and extended network. There are no family bonds that force you to stay connected.

Let's dive in.

What you've learned in this chapter:
- ***Romantic conflict is layered with attachment, intimacy, and old scripts.***
- ***Your partner is not the enemy; your nervous system and theirs are playing old roles.***
- ***The pause helps you stay present instead of spiraling.***
- ***Flip the script means choosing honesty over appeasement or control.***
- ***Clarity is the foundation of real intimacy.***

Chapter 11: Conflict with Friends and Community

"Some people arrive and make such a beautiful impact on your life, you can barely remember what life was like without them." –Anna Taylor

We expect conflict with family members. We brace for it in romantic relationships. We manage it at work. But friendship is supposed to be a safe space, an escape from all that tension, and that's exactly why it hurts so much when something breaks. When you have a rupture with a friend, especially one who is like family, it's often harder to make sense of.

There are no scripts, no social rules, no cleanup protocol. Sometimes people just fade, ghost, pretend nothing happened, or try to pick things back up without ever acknowledging the silence in between.

The grief is real because friendship is a different kind of intimacy. Friendship is the place where we laugh without performance, where we share dreams before they are formed. It's where we get to be silly and serious, lost and found, all in the same conversation. When that connection frays, it hurts not only our feelings but our sense of belonging as well.

Conflict in friendship can take so many forms. You may have a friend who falls quiet when you're struggling, or one who drains you with their constant drama. You may have outgrown a friend but feel guilty about distancing yourself from them. You may also experience a distance that sneaks in slowly—through unspoken resentment, misread texts, or a single offhand comment that triggers something deeper—yet neither of you knows how to bring it up.

Then there is community conflict: a more diffuse but equally painful tension that can unfold within a group you once trusted— your volunteer team, your spiritual circle, or your online collective. One small rupture splinters the whole thing, and suddenly the people who felt like your chosen family start to feel like strangers, or worse, like threats.

I have coached people through these moments, and I have lived them myself. Over and over again, I have seen how a friendship rupture triggers something that feels bigger than the moment. It taps into our core fear of being excluded, misunderstood, or replaced. It raises the question, *Am I too much or not enough?*

With my own friendship conflicts, I'd find myself caught in one of two patterns: chasing them down with texts or ghosting them completely.

I realized that when a friend went quiet, my brain would become a frantic storyteller, and the stories were never kind. I'd convince myself I'd been excluded or that I'd done something wrong. To stop this painful spiral, I had to create a specific practice for myself, a way to question my assumptions. I started calling it my *meaning-maker reset.*

How I Used My Meaning-Maker Reset

1. **I'd start by noticing my urge.** I'd notice that panicked desire to text them again or the familiar pull to disappear and protect myself.

2. **Then I would gently question the story.** I'd ask myself: *What am I making this silence mean? Is that story true, or is it just an old tale? What else could be going on in their life that I can't see?*

3. **Finally, I'd try to offer myself a gentler truth.** I'd say to myself: *The story I'm telling myself is that I've been rejected. A gentler possibility is that they're just overwhelmed right now.*

Let's talk about how to use the Exhale–Explore–Engage Method in these quieter heartbreaks to give you the tools to respond in a way that reflects your truth, even when the connection feels fragile.

Although not every relationship will survive conflict, the ones that do are made stronger by what you are about to learn.

Exhale: When Friendship Conflict Feels Like Rejection

When a friend pulls away, or when something shifts and no one explains why, it doesn't only sting emotionally—it hits the nervous system like a break in the safety net because connection with friends, especially chosen ones, often feels like refuge. When that connection is threatened, it can feel like exile.

And your body responds accordingly.

Your chest might tighten when a message goes unanswered, or your jaw may clench after a comment that felt sharp, even if it wasn't meant that way. You might find yourself rereading the last text thread, scanning for something you missed. Or you may do what you've always done when something feels off: go silent and disappear, hoping the tension will dissolve on its own.

⟡Ask yourself: What's your first impulse when a friend lets you down? Do you try harder? Do you apologize even when you don't know what went wrong? Do you shut down? Pretend it didn't happen?

Friendship conflict often activates older wounds. For many of us, especially those who were emotionally neglected or misunderstood growing up, peer relationships became the place where we finally felt seen. When those connections become shaky, our nervous system does not merely perceive it as disappointment; it perceives it as danger.

The impulse to react comes fast: to fix it quickly, so you don't lose them; to pull away so you don't get hurt; to apologize, even if you don't know what for.

The pause here is everything because it helps you stay with *yourself* in the uncertainty.

Pausing might be any action that disrupts the pattern in this moment: Taking a walk before replying; putting your phone down instead of sending a third message; saying out loud, "This feels activating, and I want to understand it before I respond."

The pause is what interrupts the spiral. It gives you a beat to ask:

Is this reaction coming from my present self or from the part of me that's terrified of being left behind?

Practice: Feel the Shift (in Friendship Conflict)

When something shifts in a friendship, a missed reply, a weird silence, a subtle withdrawal, your body often reacts before you do. You feel it in your chest, your gut, your throat. Something constricts. Something closes. Even if the conversation has not happened yet, your nervous system has already responded as if it has.

This is your cue to pause.

Ask:

Where do I feel this in my body?

What's happening in my breath, my shoulders, my chest?

Then do something small but anchoring:

Place your hand where it hurts or hums.

Say softly to yourself, *I feel you. I'm here.*

Touch the fabric of your sleeve, feel your feet on the floor, and take a long, slow exhale.

This does not solve the rupture, but it changes how you move through it because you have stopped ghosting yourself in the process of trying to hold on tight to the friendship.

⟡Ask yourself: When something feels off with a friend, what's the first signal your body gives you? What might it feel like to pause long enough to stay with that sensation before responding to them?

Sometimes the silence in a friendship is neutral. Someone's overwhelmed, distracted, or managing something you know nothing about.

However, when we don't pause to check in with ourselves, we fill that silence with stories, usually painful ones. The pause prevents you from being overrun by your legacy script. It enables you to feel the ache without rushing to erase it.

Explore: What Are You Making This Mean?

When a friend disappoints us, ghosts us, lashes out, or grows distant without explanation, our minds don't just register the behavior—we start telling ourselves stories about it, often without realizing what we are doing.

They don't care. I must have done something wrong. I'm too intense. They've found someone better. This always happens. I always lose people.

I once saw two friends from our group posting photos on social media from a brunch I wasn't invited to. The story my mind instantly invented was a brutal one: *They are phasing me out. I'm being replaced.*

I spent a whole day in a low-grade shame spiral. I later found out they had simply run into each other by chance. My mind had constructed an entire social rejection from a single, context-free image.

These thoughts don't come from nowhere. They come from earlier stories, maybe even from childhood times when closeness came with conditions, when loyalty was not mutual, when you were excluded, forgotten, or told you were too much or not enough. Conflict in friendships often reactivates old identities we thought we had outgrown, especially if the group makes you feel, for the first time in a long time, like you *belong*. When the connection ruptures, even gently, it can trigger internal messages we didn't know we were still carrying.

☙Ask yourself: What am I making this mean about me? What story is this stirring up about how people see me or about what I'm worth?

This is the moment to gently slow the narrative down.

Let's say a friend has not replied to your last message. Your nervous system might interpret the silence as rejection. The urge might be to double-text, apologize preemptively, withdraw, or overexplain something that didn't even happen.

The Exhale–Explore–Engage Method invites you to *get curious instead*.

When friendship conflict hits, it rarely feels logical. It feels personal. Raw. Sometimes confusingly disproportionate. That's often because it activates an old part of you that remembers what it felt like to be left out, replaced, or misunderstood.

I had to learn to investigate this for myself. When a friendship conflict felt illogical or disproportionately painful, I knew it wasn't about the present moment. It was about history.

I started using the *find the pattern* practice to figure out who, exactly, was feeling so hurt. This is what it looks like.

Practice: Find the Pattern (in Friendship + Community)
Step 1: Spot the part
Who just got activated?

Is it the Over-giver? The One Who Fears Rejection Before It Happens? The One Who Believes Silence Equals Abandonment? Just naming a part can help you see that it's not all of you. It's a part of you trying to stay safe.

Step 2: Ask what it's protecting
What is this part afraid might happen if I don't respond the usual way?
Sometimes it's afraid of being forgotten. Sometimes it's trying to avoid another round of invisible labor. Sometimes it just does not want to be the one who cares more. These fears are often old, yet their grip can still feel current.

Step 3: Trace the pattern and reconnect with self
Where might I have learned this script?
What would my grounded self say to this part right now?
This is not about dragging yourself through emotional history; it's about letting it whisper just long enough to soften. Then comes the return, not as the Abandoned Child or the Fixer, but as the Self who can choose to respond with clarity.

⟡***Ask yourself: What part of you reacts hardest when friendship feels uncertain? What's it afraid of losing? What might it feel like to let it know: "Thank you for protecting me, but I've got this one."***

What Friendship Conflict Often Reveals

When someone close to you pulls away or miscommunicates, it's rarely about the thing that happened. It's about what was *not* said. It's about mismatched expectations, misread intentions, and vulnerability thresholds that didn't align.

If you are someone who values connection deeply, who often shows up with your whole heart, you may unconsciously take on more responsibility than is yours.

I have coached many people through these moments. One client, Mia, was heartbroken when her friend of ten years stopped reaching out.

There was no big fight, no final blow, only a gradual fading away. Mia's first instinct was to spiral into self-doubt. When she explored what the silence was triggering, she realized it was not only about her friend; it was about feeling discarded, as if she'd been growing, but no one wanted to grow *with* her. The pain was not only about the absence of contact—it was the fear that her truth had become too heavy for the people who once felt like home.

◯ **Try this:** When friendship feels shaky, journal the sentence: *This makes me feel...* Then follow it with: *What I'm afraid this means about me is...* Notice what parts of you still carry old fear and what they need from you now.

The goal here is not to resolve the dynamic, but to *see it clearly*—both the other person's behavior and your own inner experience. Once you understand the pattern you are in, you can stop trying to fix what was never yours to carry.

Engage: Repair, Reset, or Release

Once you've exhaled and explored what this conflict is bringing up, slowing the loop of self-doubt or silent blame, you're ready to engage.

In friendship conflict, however, engaging does not always mean confrontation. Sometimes the most honest next step is *repair*. Other times, it's *recalibration* or *resetting the terms*. Occasionally, it's *release*.

The Exhale–Explore–Engage Method does not assume that every relationship can or should be saved, but it does ask you to respond from a place of honesty, not from urgency, fear, or old scripts.

Flip the Script: Rewriting the Story of Friendship Conflict

Friendship conflict carries a particular kind of ache. It's not always loud, but it's unmistakably sharp. There's no legal tie or family obligation; what exists instead is history, vulnerability, and shared memory. That makes the decision to engage, and how to do so, a uniquely delicate one.

Flipping the script in friendship, I learned, doesn't always mean saving the relationship. Sometimes it means choosing a response that restores self-respect.

After years of either chasing clarity or disappearing altogether, I knew I needed a new way. I had to learn how to *flip the script* in a way that felt honest and true to *myself*, even if the outcome was uncertain.

Step 1: Name your default

What do I usually do when something feels off with a friend?

Do you chase clarity? Go silent and hope it passes? Pretend it does not hurt? Do you overextend to prove your worth? Start by noticing the role you typically play in the script you've been cast in.

Step 2: Flip it, and expand it

What would be the opposite of that?

What are two other responses I could try?

If you usually overexplain, try one simple sentence. If you usually ghost: try saying, "This dynamic feels different. Can we talk about it?"

Other options:

"I want to understand what changed. Are you open to a conversation?"

"I have noticed I have been holding a lot in this friendship. Can I be honest about that?"

When exploring the opposite move, remember the guardrail we set earlier. With friends, where the fear of being excluded runs deep, the aim is the constructive opposite. If your pattern is to go quiet and make yourself small, the opposite isn't to become demanding or aggressive; it's to find a response that allows you to stay true to yourself without abandoning the possibility of connection.

Step 3: Try each one in your body

Imagine saying each one, then ask yourself, *Where do I feel resistance? Where do I feel a flicker of level-headedness or relief?*

That's the *body yes*, the option that may be uncomfortable but still feels honest.

Step 4: Choose the one that aligns

Choose the response that honors who you are becoming, not who you've been in past friendships. Choose the one that leaves you feeling like you showed up for yourself and your friendship, even if things don't get resolved. Sometimes flipping the script in friendship is about speaking. Sometimes it's about stepping back. Either way, it's not about winning. It's about walking away with your integrity intact.

♡Think of a friendship where something shifted, but you stayed silent. What was your default? What would a more honest, less rehearsed response sound like now?

Sometimes flipping the script is not enough, and it may be helpful to step back and think about your goals for the relationship. You might have already flipped the script a few times, responded differently, but it's still not a fulfilling relationship that brings you joy.

♡Ask yourself: What am I hoping for here? Do I want reconnection? Clarity? Peace? Distance?

Your answer will help you choose the kind of engagement that reflects your integrity.

Option 1: Repair

Sometimes the Exhale–Explore–Engage Method is reaching out—not to perform reconciliation, but to invite an honest conversation. This doesn't require perfection or a masterful script. Just courage and clarity.

Try this script: "Hey, I've been sitting with our last conversation. I miss you, and I also feel like something's unresolved. If you are open to talking, I'd love to check in."

Or: "I've noticed some distance between us. I don't want to make assumptions, but I value our friendship and would like to reconnect if it feels mutual."

Case Study: Reconnecting with Grace

One client, Sophie, had a close friend she hadn't spoken to in nearly a year after a miscommunication that neither of them had addressed. The silence stretched into awkwardness. After doing her work, Sophie reached out—not with blame or a need for a perfect resolution, but with a simple truth: "I miss you. I know things got weird. If you ever want to talk, I'm here."

They met for coffee. It wasn't an immediate repair, but it was a beginning, and it happened because she spoke from presence, not pressure.

Option 2: Reset the terms

Sometimes the friendship does not need to end, but it does need to change. Perhaps you've realized you can no longer be their emotional emergency contact or that your energy is depleted by one-sided effort. In these moments, the Exhale–Explore–Engage Method is about *adjusting your availability*, not cutting them off.

Try this script: "I love you, and I also need to show up for myself differently these days. I want to stay close, but I might not have the same bandwidth I used to."

Or: "I value you, and I also need us to talk about what's been feeling off between us." This is especially useful in friend groups, spiritual communities, or volunteer circles where clarity can be a gift.

Case Study: Boundaries Without Goodbye

A client named Noah found himself playing therapist in his friend circle. Everyone came to him with their breakdowns, but when he needed support, no one followed up. He didn't want to end the friendships, but he did not want to keep overextending himself either. So he started saying things like: "I'm here to listen, but I can only hold space for a bit right now" and "That sounds hard. Have you talked to someone who can support you?"

At first, people were surprised, but eventually they came to respect the shift. And Noah stopped feeling like he had to abandon himself to be loved.

Option 3: Release with integrity

Sometimes the clearest response is to let go—not with drama, but with dignity. Not all endings need lengthy explanations, but the

Exhale–Explore–Engage Method offers a gentle path for conscious release.

Try this if you feel closure is needed: "I have appreciated our friendship, and I have also been feeling like we're in different places lately. I'm letting go of trying to force what does not feel aligned anymore. I wish you well." Sometimes no words are needed. You can disengage not from avoidance, but from self-respect. The absence of reactivity *is* the choice.

Case Study: The Quiet Ending

Maya, a client who had grown close to someone in a wellness community, started noticing that the friendship was rooted in constant venting, gossip, and emotional dependency. She tried bringing it up. Nothing changed. So she slowly stopped engaging. She didn't ghost. She just stepped back. She didn't make it a "big thing." She made it *true*. Even though it hurt, she told me later: "It's the first time I didn't betray myself to stay connected."

⟡*Think about a friendship or group dynamic that feels out of alignment. Which third option are you being called into: repair, reset, or release? What would engaging from clarity (not conditioning) look like?*

There's a reason we don't talk enough about friendship conflict. It feels ambiguous. Less "justified." It may be harder to name, but the grief that comes from a ruptured friendship or a community that no longer feels like home is every bit as real as any breakup. Sometimes more so because you didn't see it coming or because you never thought you'd have to choose between connection and your well-being.

While there can never be any guarantees for reconnection with others, the Exhale–Explore–Engage Method gives you a way to move through the mess without betraying yourself. It allows you to speak gently when silence has gone on for too long. It gives you permission to set boundaries in relationships where none were expected. It also helps you leave when the connection no longer reflects who you are. An authentic connection does not require forced effort or resolving every conflict. True peace and renewed closeness arise from simply being present in each moment. No matter where the conflict arises, whether at home, with others, or deep within ourselves, the path to clarity remains the same: pause, be curious, and choose a response that reflects your truth.

What you've learned in this chapter:
- ***Friendship rupture often awakens core fears of exclusion or abandonment.***
- ***Your stories ("They don't care" / "I messed up") deserve recognition.***
- ***Whether you choose to repair, reset, or release, your options are wider than you think.***
- ***Flip the script allows you to step out of chasing or ghosting.***
- ***Integrity in friendship means being honest about capacity, needs, and change.***

Chapter 12: Conflict at Work

"We don't rise to the level of our goals. We fall to the level of our systems." –James Clear

Workplace conflict is where "let's circle back on that" can mean anything from "I genuinely need more time" to "I'd rather juggle flaming porcupines than discuss this with you right now." Work is where we spend a staggering amount of our time, energy, and attention. It's where we show up to build, lead, contribute, and, if we're lucky, grow. It's also one of the most emotionally charged arenas for conflict because the stakes are high, the dynamics are layered, and the cost of getting it "wrong" can feel enormous.

At work, we don't just fear rejection; we fear losing credibility. We worry about our future, our performance reviews, and our reputations. Conflict here can threaten not only a relationship but our livelihood. Unlike family or romantic relationships, where there is (usually) room for repair, the workplace can be far less forgiving. There is a silent pressure to keep things professional, which is often code for *don't show too much emotion; don't take things personally; don't have a human response to an inhuman system.*

Despite these professional dictums, conflict at work still affects us on a personal level. It touches your sense of identity, worth, and safety. When someone criticizes your idea in a meeting, when a teammate takes credit for your work, or when your boss micromanages or goes silent, it doesn't just feel frustrating; it can feel like a threat. When you don't have the tools or the permission to process that threat, you end up carrying it in your body: in clenched jaws, racing thoughts, endless ruminations, and 3 a.m. drafts of emails you'll never send.

I once worked with a client (let's call her Margaret) who led a high-performing team in a growing company. On paper, she had it all—influence, autonomy, a great track record—but she kept hitting the same wall. When disagreements happened, especially with her leadership team, she'd go quiet. Numb. Her ideas would disappear from the room because she couldn't bring herself to speak. "I just freeze," she told me. "I know I should say something. I just can't." Upon tracing it back, we found that it was not a strategy problem. It was a safety problem. Conflict in her childhood meant chaos. So even as a successful adult, her nervous system didn't distinguish between a tense meeting and a relational rupture.

Conflict at work does not start at work. It begins in our wiring— in our roles and our histories. We bring all of it to the office, even if we're dressed in blazers and speaking in PowerPoint. Unless we know how to recognize the signs, we'll mistake the tension for something we should avoid when it's actually an invitation to get curious about ourselves.

Think of a recent moment of tension at work. Was there something you wanted to say but didn't? What stopped you? If you trace that reaction back, does it remind you of something older, something that didn't start in your job at all?

Exhale: What Impulse Looks Like at Work

In work conflicts, the first reaction often occurs before you even realize a line has been crossed. There is a subtle shift in tone, a poorly worded email, a passive-aggressive comment in a meeting, and suddenly your body, no longer in "collaborate" mode, is primed and ready to protect you.

When conflict happens in the workplace, the reaction does not always look explosive. You don't scream, cry, or walk out. Instead, your impulse gets compressed into something more "acceptable." You might go silent, overapologize, or rehearse your response a dozen times in your head without ever saying it out loud. You may find yourself overcompensating with extra work, making the slide deck perfect, or staying late even though no one asked you to.

It's easy to miss that this response is also an impulse, because in the workplace our first reactions don't always look like reactions. Sometimes they look like productivity. I was a master of this. After one tense review with a manager, I didn't argue or complain; I went back to my desk and created the most beautiful, color-coded, data-rich spreadsheet the company had ever seen. On the surface, I was a great employee. In reality, my nervous system was screaming, *See? I'm valuable! Please don't fire me!* My panic was channeled directly into a pivot table.

For one of my clients, Owen, a product manager at a fast-moving tech company, his instinct was to defuse tension by rushing in to fix everything, even when it wasn't his mess to clean up. "If there is silence after a bad meeting," he told me, "I'll be the first to send a follow-up. I'll smooth it over. I'll offer solutions." Underneath the initiative was panic. His body felt the tension as a danger, and his urge was to neutralize it quickly.

This is why the pause is so essential at work, as it allows you to lead from clarity, not reflex.

Practice: Feel the Shift (at Work)

In the workplace, your body often registers tension long before your brain can justify it. It responds to a client's curt feedback, a colleague's subtle dismissal, a change in someone's tone. Suddenly, without conscious awareness, your breath shortens, your chest tightens, and your hands hover over the keyboard trying to word that message "just right."

That's the shift. The moment when your nervous system says, *This does not feel safe.*

Pause right there.

Instead of overcorrecting or overperforming, take a beat to tune into your body

Place your hand on your chest or belly. Ask: *What's happening in here right now?*

Feel the urge to please, defend, or disappear, and name it as a response, not a requirement.

Exhale slowly. Let one breath become a placeholder for a better response later.

You don't need to say anything yet. You don't need to solve it. You only need to stay with yourself so you don't abandon your clarity before the conversation even begins.

Next time you feel a heat rise during a meeting, a tightening after an email, or a sudden shutdown in your voice, what would it look like to stay in contact with your body for three breaths before doing anything at all?

This is not about detachment or delay. It's about choosing. If you speak from the first impulse, you might say something that sounds polished but costs you your peace. Maybe even something you will later regret saying.

If you act out of habit, you might maintain the peace by simply disappearing. Yet when you pause, even for five seconds, you create just enough room for something else. Something more grounded. Something more for you.

Explore: What's This Really About?

Work conflict rarely begins and ends at the surface. It might look like a disagreement about project scope, a passive-aggressive comment in a team thread, or a colleague talking over you in a meeting. Underneath those moments is usually something else— something personal, emotional, and often unspoken. This step is designed to help you uncover the story behind the sting.

Let's say your boss gives last-minute feedback on a presentation you worked hard on. You feel your chest tighten and your stomach drop. The urge to defend yourself rises fast, maybe in your head, maybe out loud. If you pause and get curious, you might notice the voice behind the reaction: *They don't respect my time. I'm never enough. If I don't get this right, I'll lose my value.*

These aren't work issues. They are worthiness issues, and they usually didn't start at work.

Internal Family Systems offers a powerful way to understand this: The parts of you reacting at work are often much younger than they seem. That perfectionist voice scrambling to fix the slide deck before 9 a.m.? It's the part that learned early on that being helpful meant being safe. That freeze response when someone questions your decision in front of others? It's the part that remembers how it felt to be blamed unfairly as a kid. Each part of you has a reason. A memory. A story that does not want to be repeated.

Practice: Find the Pattern (in Workplace Conflict)

Work conflict rarely activates your whole self. More often, it activates a well-rehearsed part of you, one that learned long ago that competence = safety or invisibility = protection.

Step 1: Spot the part

Who's speaking right now?

Is it the Fixer? The Overachiever? The part that believes one misstep will cost you everything? You don't need a label, just enough recognition to know *this is a pattern.*

Step 2: Ask what it's protecting

What does this part think it's saving me from?

Maybe it's shame, exposure, or being seen as incompetent. Sometimes just asking this question shifts the energy inside you. You realize *this is not about this project; it's about an old fear.*

Step 3: Trace the pattern and reconnect to Self

Where did I learn this was the only safe way to respond?

This is not about going back to dwell in that space where you first learned to respond this way, it's about going back to retrieve the part of you that got stuck there. Once that part feels seen, your wiser voice can step in: *Thank you. I know you're trying to help, but I can handle this differently now.*

♡Ask yourself: What's your most practiced pattern at work? What is it trying to prevent? How might your presence, not your performance, be enough in this moment?

One client, Anika, a VP in a high-stakes startup, used to feel paralyzed when a particular senior colleague questioned her in meetings. She thought it was intimidation. In our sessions, however, she uncovered an old story: as a teenager, her father would grill her on details, and she never had the correct answer. Her urge to go blank was not a sign of incompetence; it was a form of protection. Once she recognized this, she didn't need to overprepare or avoid the colleague. She just needed to ground herself in the present and remember that she was no longer fifteen.

♡Think of a time you felt small at work. What part of you was reacting? What story was it trying to protect you from reliving?

The goal of the **Explore** step is not to psychoanalyze every office annoyance. The goal is to create enough space to notice that what's happening in the moment isn't what your nervous system is sounding the alarm about. Because once you become aware of the story, you can start letting it go.

Engage: Choosing From Truth at Work

Work conflict does not always show up in big, dramatic moments. Sometimes it arrives in a calendar invite that makes your stomach drop. A team message that feels passive-aggressive. A sudden tightness in your jaw during a meeting when someone takes credit for your idea, again.

At work, your legacy patterns often take on their most effective disguise. You don't yell. You don't slam doors. You "stay professional." Inside, your nervous system is reading the room just as fast as it does at home. The same impulse to fix, fawn, freeze, or flee still lives in your body—and if you've done a good job surviving workplace tension over the years, those reactions may look polished, calm, even admirable. But they still come at a cost because they weren't chosen from clarity. They were inherited or practiced.

That's where **Engage** comes in. Not to push you toward confrontation, but to guide you back to the version of yourself who can respond intentionally. After the pause and the inquiry, you stand at a critical fork in the road. One path feels familiar: the one you always take, keeping things smooth and nonconfrontational, telling you to smile, nod, fix it yourself, or "circle back later." The other path, while potentially awkward or counterintuitive, is the one that reflects your clarity.

Flip the Script: Choosing Clarity in the Workplace

For years, I defaulted to patterns that looked polished but left me feeling disconnected and resentful. I would overfunction, stay quiet, or carry the emotional weight of the entire team. I had to find a way to *flip the script*—to choose a response that reflected my clarity, not just my conditioning. Engaging meant practicing being internally aligned in a system that often encouraged me to abandon myself. Flipping the script at work means reclaiming your voice without abandoning your professionalism or your truth.

Step 1: Name your default

What do I usually do when things get tense at work?

Do you stay quiet? Overexplain? Say "yes" when you mean "no"? Soften your ideas? Circle back later and hope it goes away? Name what you do. Kindly. Clearly. It's how you begin to intervene.

Step 2: Flip it and expand it

What would the opposite look like?

What are two more responses I haven't tried?

If you usually appease, could you ask a boundary-setting question? If you usually stay silent, could you name your concern? If you usually say yes, could you say, "I'd like to pause and revisit this with more clarity" or "Here's what I think works, and here's what does not."

The point is not to do this perfectly. It's merely to interrupt the loop. And remember the guardrail we set. In the workplace, where the cost of getting it "wrong" feels enormous, the aim is always the *constructive opposite*. If your pattern is to appease or avoid conflict to protect your reputation, the opposite isn't to become confrontational and burn bridges. It's to find a response that allows you to advocate for your work with clarity and integrity.

Step 3: Try each option in your body

Imagine saying each response in a meeting, in a reply email, or across the table. Then ask: Which one lets your spine lengthen? Which one softens your breath? Which one makes you feel a little more like yourself? That's your *body yes*, a physiological cue that can tell you which option is good for you.

Step 4: Choose the one that aligns

Choose the response that holds both your professionalism and your truth. The one that lets you be kind without abandoning yourself.

Flipping the script at work is not about proving a point; it's about practicing internal alignment in an external system. It's about remembering that you have a right to clarity, too.

⟡Think of a recent moment when you defaulted to politeness, overworking, or passivity. What else could you have tried? What would it look like to choose something small, but more aligned, next time?

Case Study: Saying the Thing You Never Say

Taylor, a senior program manager, had a long history of being "the glue" on her team. She ran meetings, soothed egos, and picked up the slack. Over time, she began to resent how invisible her contributions had become. During one particularly tense cross-functional meeting, a colleague cut her off while she was presenting. She felt the usual reaction: shrink, smile, move on. Then, something shifted. She paused, took a breath, and remembered her value.

"I'd like to finish the thought," she said, calm but firm. "I spent a lot of time preparing this update, and I think it's worth hearing."

No one gasped. The world didn't end. But something profound happened inside her. She heard herself speak from clarity instead of reaction. She felt her feet on the floor. Her voice was steady. She didn't override herself. The conversation that followed was more collaborative, not less.

Case Study: The Quiet Leader Who Found His Voice

John, a director at a fast-scaling startup, often felt stuck between advocating for his team and appeasing leadership. In one executive meeting, he found himself nodding along with a decision he didn't support.

He noticed his body went cold, and instead of staying silent, he paused and said, "I need a minute to reflect before I agree to this. Can we come back to it?"

It was awkward. He felt exposed, but that pause gave him time to check his integrity. Later, when he returned to the conversation, he was able to propose an alternative that respected his team's bandwidth *and* aligned with leadership's goals. No drama. Just leadership from alignment.

⟁ *Think of a recent moment at work where you felt yourself go quiet, override your truth, or get pulled into an old role. What would the Exhale–Explore–Engage Method have looked like in that moment?*

Engage is not always about saying something bold. Sometimes it's about *not* rescuing the conversation. Sometimes it's choosing not to interrupt yourself. Sometimes it's allowing a little tension in the room so that something truer can emerge.

Conflict at work is not only the clashing of ideas; it's about identities, roles, and unspoken agreements. It's about power and protection, visibility and value, and it's one of the places where our oldest patterns can show up wearing their sharpest suits.

What you've begun to practice here, the Exhale–Explore–Engage Method, is not just useful in hard conversations. It's transformational because it teaches you to stay connected to yourself in a space that feels uncomfortable or even intense.

When you pause before jumping in, get curious about what's underneath, and respond from clarity instead of habit, you start changing more than your tone. You change your presence. You show up as someone who can handle discomfort without abandoning yourself. You begin leading, even if you don't have the title for it. And you do it without sacrificing your health, your voice, or your truth.

That's what the Exhale–Explore–Engage Method makes possible at work. Not perfect interactions but aligned ones. When you start showing up that way, you give others permission to do the same.

◯Ask yourself: What's one interaction at work where I can plan to practice this next? It doesn't have to be high stakes. It just has to be real.

Most of us can find our way back to connection after a disagreement. We've been practicing. We're learning to pause, to explore, and to engage from a place of clarity rather than old conditioning. But what happens when the other person does not— or cannot—meet you there?

What do you do when the conflict does not feel like a one-off but like a pattern that never ends? What do you do when everything you say is twisted, when you're constantly walking on eggshells, when empathy is met with blame, and boundaries are met with escalation?

Remember, the Exhale–Explore–Engage Method is always available to you, *even when others don't operate from the same framework.* When you encounter individuals who thrive on conflict, seem allergic to accountability, or repeatedly pull you into chaos, the work shifts from simply staying present to actively protecting your peace while fiercely guarding your truth.

That's what we'll explore next.

What you've learned in this chapter:

- *Professional roles can mask emotional patterns, but the body still reacts.*
- *You can stay calm yet still be abandoning yourself.*
- *The pause gives you time to choose professionalism that's real, not performative.*
- *Flip the script helps you say the thing you never say from a place of grounded clarity.*
- *Internal alignment builds external authority, especially in moments of tension.*

Chapter 13: Dealing With High-Conflict Personalities

"You can't reason someone out of a position they didn't reason themselves into." –Jonathan Swift

With some people in your life, no matter how much work you do on yourself, how thoughtful your communication, how generous your assumptions, or how many times you try to start fresh, the pattern does not budge. You pause. You breathe. You show up with clarity. Yet still, you find yourself pulled back into a familiar loop: blame, defensiveness, emotional chaos, walking on eggshells.

Some people don't merely have conflict *with* others; they create conflict *around* them. For them, conflict is often a way of regulating, controlling, or gaining attention, power, and validation. These are the individuals that Bill Eddy, therapist and founder of the High Conflict Institute, refers to as "high-conflict personalities."

High-conflict personalities aren't just difficult or dramatic. What sets them apart is the repetition and the pattern. You can feel it in your body after enough interactions. Nothing gets resolved, and nothing really changes. The moment you set a boundary, they escalate. The moment you let your guard down, they twist your words. There is no shared middle ground, just a cycle of reactivity that runs until you are exhausted, confused, and doubting your version of events.

A Crucial Safety Note: As we discuss how to manage these challenging dynamics, it's vital to remember the core principle established in the introduction: Your safety is ALWAYS the priority. The Exhale–Explore–Engage Method is not a tool for situations involving abuse, harassment, or physical or psychological danger. If you are in a situation where you feel unsafe, the goal is not to engage but to get to safety and seek help from appropriate sources (see Bonus Materials for the list of resources).

According to Eddy's research and clinical practice, most high-conflict people share four key traits:

1. **Blaming**: They rarely take responsibility and almost always find someone else to blame.
2. **All-or-nothing thinking**: You are either with them or against them. Right or wrong. Angel or enemy.
3. **Unmanaged emotions**: Their feelings drive their behavior, often leading to impulsive or extreme reactions.
4. **Extreme behaviors**: This can range from verbal abuse to ghosting, emotional blackmail, public outbursts, or silent treatment.

They may seem charismatic or wounded, crying one moment and raging the next. While some look like bullies and others like martyrs, the through line is this: When conflict arises, they don't regulate—they escalate.

If you are a sensitive, thoughtful person who *wants* to do better in conflict, someone who reflects, apologizes, and tries to meet people where they are, these dynamics can be particularly devastating. Your empathy becomes the hook. Your willingness to repair becomes the leash. Suddenly, you are stuck in a dynamic where their chaos sets the tempo, and your nervous system can't seem to find steady ground.

This does not mean these people are incapable of change, but it does mean that *your inner work alone won't fix the dynamic.* No matter how many times you pause, explore, and try to engage differently, if the other person is unwilling or unable to meet you in this work, *you may be faced with making a choice that prioritizes your own well-being.*

♡*Think of someone in your life who always seems to pull you into conflict, even when you try to avoid it. Do you recognize any of the four traits: blaming, all-or-nothing thinking, unmanaged emotions, and extreme behaviors? How do you tend to respond, and how does your body feel afterward?*

Exhale: When Conflict Feels Like a Trap

Dealing with a high-conflict person rarely feels like a simple disagreement; it feels like a trap where any kind of resolution seems impossible. The moment their tone shifts, your words are twisted, or they go from zero to sixty over something small, and your body reacts before your brain even has time to register what's happening. You might feel your stomach flip, your chest tighten, or your jaw set as you brace for impact. It can feel like walking into a room of land mines; your entire system starts scanning for danger.

⟁Think of someone in your life who fits the high-conflict pattern. What happens in your body when they start to push your buttons? Do you lean in to argue, shut down, overexplain, or walk on eggshells to prevent further escalation?

For many of my clients, the most common impulses in these situations are:

To defend ("That's not what I said!")

To explain ("Here's why I did it that way...")

To appease ("Okay, I'll just fix it.")

To shut down completely ("Nothing I say will help.")

These aren't conscious strategies; they are nervous system reflexes. When someone comes at you with blame, distortion, or drama, it's not a typical conversation anymore. It's survival mode.

In high-conflict dynamics, the impulse to respond fast and emotionally is even stronger than usual. That's because high-conflict people tend to operate from a place of emotional reactivity themselves.

Their communication style triggers your stress response because your body recognizes that this is not safe ground. Even if the topic is small, the stakes feel high. There is usually a history of unpredictability, volatility, or disproportionate responses that your body has catalogued. And it remembers them all too well.

Exhaling is the first and most radical step.

When I work with clients stuck in high-conflict dynamics, the first thing we practice is not what to say but how to stay grounded in their bodies when the internal alarm bells sound. I explain that before they can engage differently, they first have to learn to feel that shift without getting swept away by it. This practice is their foundational anchor.

My First Instruction: Feel the Shift

Here is the first process I guide my clients through:

1. **I ask them to notice the first physical cue.** When that person starts to push their buttons, what is the very first thing that changes? Do their shoulders tense? Does their breath vanish? Do they feel pressure to respond immediately? That is the signal.

2. **Then, I suggest a small, grounding action.** I might have them place a hand on their chest or thigh—anywhere that helps them feel anchored in the present moment, not in the chaos of the drama that's unfolding.

3. **Finally, we focus on one slow exhale.** I remind them, "Urgency is not clarity. You are allowed to pause for a moment." This single breath is what begins to bring their thinking brain back online.

⟡Ask yourself: What's your earliest physical cue that you are being pulled into someone else's storm? What would it feel like to stay with that sensation without obeying it?

Let your nervous system register that *you are safe*. You are uncomfortable, sure. You are being challenged, maybe unfairly, but you're not in any immediate *danger*, and that distinction is what gives you access to your higher brain functions again.

I often tell clients to build in "micropauses" when dealing with high-conflict people. It could be one deep breath before answering. A short phrase like "Let me think about that," a delay in replying to a text or email, even just standing up and moving your body—or putting your hand on your chest, and feeling the ground beneath your feet.

The goal is not to avoid the conversation. It's to avoid reacting from the same part of you that's been provoked. It's time to step out of the tug-of-war long enough to remember that you don't want to win, you just want clarity, peace, and self-respect.

⟡Think of a recent conversation with a high-conflict person where you felt hijacked. If you could rewind that moment, where would you insert a pause? What kind of breath, movement, or phrase might have helped you disrupt the urgency?

This is the moment the Exhale–Explore–Engage Method begins: not with the perfect response, but with the courage not to respond right away.

Explore: What's This Really About?

When you are dealing with someone who seems wired for conflict—who blames, escalates, rewrites reality, or keeps coming back for another round—you can easily get swept into the storm. It's not just what they say; it's how it lands. Fast. Sharp. Sometimes absurd. And when your nervous system gets hooked, the urge is to defend, explain, correct, or retreat.

If you can pause long enough to ask, *What's this really about?*—not only for them, but for you—you begin to shift the dynamic entirely.

High-conflict personalities often provoke more than just frustration. They stir something deeper. For many of us, they echo dynamics we've known before: the volatile parent, the unpredictable partner, the boss who kept moving the goalposts.

So the first invitation in this step is not to analyze the other person, it's to explore the part of you that feels activated in their presence.

⟠Ask yourself: When they lash out, what story does your brain start to tell you? Are you failing? Are you unsafe? Are you about to be abandoned or humiliated?

This step is where we investigate the pattern to understand the *loop*.

Inner Mapping with Parts

According to Internal Family Systems, what we call *overreactions* are often younger parts of us taking the wheel. These are parts that learned early on that safety means staying agreeable, explaining quickly, or avoiding conflict at any cost.

Let's say a co-parent sends a barrage of accusatory texts. You feel a fire in your chest, and your fingers hover over your keyboard. A part of you wants to hit back. Another wants to explain. A third wants to say nothing and disappear.

Practice: Find the Pattern (In High-Conflict Dynamics)

These interactions don't just pull you into a state of reactivity; they pull you into legacy scripts. Your response may feel exaggerated because the part of you that steps forward has been here before.

Step 1: Spot the part

Who just stepped in to manage this?

Is this the part that smooths things over to keep the peace? The one that overexplains in hopes of being understood? The version of you that fawns, flares, or freezes? Just naming the part can give you enough distance to lead with Self-energy instead of being dragged along.

Step 2: Ask what it's protecting

What is this part trying to prevent?

Sometimes it's shame. Sometimes it's chaos. Sometimes it's the old terror of not being believed or taken seriously. Ask the part, *What are you afraid would happen if I didn't respond this way?*

Step 3: Trace the pattern and reconnect with Self

Where did I learn this response?

You might remember a parent who never let things be calm, a teacher who shamed you into staying quiet, or a boss who manipulated your loyalty. Whatever surfaces, thank the part for protecting you back then and gently let it know *I'm the one driving now.*

⬭ ***Ask yourself: Which part of you gets hooked by this person again and again? What's it afraid of? What would it need to hear to step back even a little?***

This inner mapping does not have to be formal or time-consuming; even thirty seconds can shift your posture from reactivity to curiosity, making everything else possible.

Loosening the Hook

In high-conflict interactions, it's easy to mistake the feeling of urgency for importance. The louder and more intense the other person becomes, the more compelled we feel to match their emotional level. This is precisely the trap.

Bill Eddy teaches that responding with empathy, attention, and respect—without engaging in blame, emotion, or argument—can de-escalate the interaction, but that's nearly impossible if your internal system is in a state of panic. So exploring your own *hook* is critical.

My hook was always the need to be seen as *reasonable*. I once spent an entire hour on the phone with a family member, calmly trying to explain my perspective while they grew increasingly emotional and accusatory. I walked away feeling completely drained, as if I'd run a marathon. I realized later that by trying to be reasonable, I had volunteered to be the container for their chaos. The moment I decided my peace was more important than their approval, the hook lost its power.

Perhaps your hook is the belief that you must prove your point. Or that if you don't respond, you'll lose credibility. Or that keeping the peace is your responsibility. Each of those hooks could benefit from a gentle interrogation: *Is this true? Where did I learn this? What would happen if I didn't respond that way right now?*

This process is not about spiritual bypassing or pretending the other person is not harmful. It's about finding a posture that protects your peace without collapsing your boundaries. These small, compassionate pauses create room for something different to emerge; you can listen without reacting and reflect without losing yourself. That's what **Explore** makes possible, and from that space, you'll be ready to choose how you want to **Engage**—not from fear or reflex, but from clarity and power.

Engage: Choosing from Clarity

When you are dealing with someone who thrives on intensity, who seems to escalate every conversation, twist your words, or create chaos no matter how calmly you try to respond, the Exhale–Explore–Engage Method becomes more than a tool—it's a lifeline.

By the time you reach this step, you've already done something many people never do: You've paused. You've interrupted your instinct to retaliate, retreat, or rescue. You've listened to the alarm underneath your discomfort. Now, instead of walking straight into the same old dysfunctional dance, you get to ask: *What does engagement look like when I'm rooted in clarity, not reactivity?*

Remember that engagement does not mean agreement. It also does not mean fixing the situation, proving your point, or convincing the other person to see your side. It means responding in a way that protects your peace and reflects your values, *not their chaos*.

1. Calm, contained, and clear

High-conflict people tend to be reactive, black-and-white thinkers who blame others and struggle with emotional regulation. When they escalate, your best tool is not logic. It's containment. One powerful way to do this is through what I call the *three Cs of clarity* (inspired by Bill Eddy's BIFF method):

Be Concise: The fewer words, the better. Say what you need to say. No explanations, no defending.

Be Compassionate: Be respectful without trying to please. You're not responsible for their reaction.

Be Clear: State boundaries, decisions, or facts simply. Avoid getting pulled into debating interpretations.

A co-parenting client, Chelsea, kept getting emotionally charged emails from her ex. The pattern was familiar: long, accusatory rants followed by guilt-tripping about the kids. Her old pattern was to respond with point-by-point rebuttals.

After practicing the Exhale–Explore–Engage Method, her new reply was: "Thanks for your input. I'll stick with the current plan and revisit next week. Let me know if anything urgent comes up with the kids." There was no heat, no hook, no fuel for the fire. At first, it felt almost robotic, but the profound relief she felt afterward, with her heart calm and no endless replaying of the email in her head, was when she knew it was working.

2. Respond to the future, not the drama

A key strategy when dealing with high-conflict personalities is to *shift the focus to the future*. These personalities often fixate on blame, past grievances, and emotional injury. Instead of getting dragged back, redirect the conversation toward what's next.

Try phrases like:

"What's your proposed plan moving forward?"

"We can revisit the past another time. Right now, let's look at the next step."

"Let's talk about what's possible going forward."

These kinds of responses help defuse the drama.

One client, a manager named Priya, had a team member who constantly stirred up interpersonal drama and deflected responsibility. Instead of feeding the loop, she started each conversation with: "Before we get into how we got here, tell me how you want this to be resolved."

This simple sentence changed the energy. The employee was forced to think ahead, not stew in blame.

3. Set boundaries, not ultimatums

With high-conflict personalities, boundaries are essential, but they need to be calm, consistent, and enforceable. You can state, "This is the limit. If you go through the red, there is a consequence." Instead of saying, "You always do this. If you don't stop, I'm done," try saying, "I won't continue this conversation if the tone remains disrespectful. We can revisit it when things are calmer." The boundary is *about you*, not about controlling them. It centers your agency.

✐Write a list of the three most common conflict situations you face with this person. For each one, define:
- o   Your boundary.
- o   The consequence you can and *will* enforce.
- o   A short, clear sentence to communicate it.

4. Don't overexplain, don't defend

Try this tool: The BIFF prep (developed by Bill Eddy). Prepare a short, clear, nonreactive message using the brief, informative, friendly, firm (Bill Eddy's BIFF method).

Instructions:

1. **Brief:** 1–2 sentences max.
2. **Informative:** Share facts, not feelings.
3. **Friendly:** Neutral, not cold.
4. **Firm:** Close the loop and don't invite more drama.

Example: "Thanks for the update. I'll respond once I have reviewed the schedule. I won't be available for further discussion this weekend."

This blend of acknowledgment + boundary is often enough to diffuse the emotional charge, if only slightly. Even a slight shift creates space for you to stay in your power.

Flip the Script: Holding Your Ground Without Losing Yourself

High-conflict people want you in a role. They elicit the Overexplainer, the Fixer, the one who stays quiet to keep the peace, or escalates so they can blame you for the blow-up. When you flip the script in these relationships, you don't just disrupt the dynamic. You reclaim your clarity.

Here is what flipping the script looks like in a relationship with a high-conflict personality: not trying to fix or connect, but choosing a response that protects your clarity, your nervous system, and your time. It means stepping out of the role they expect you to play, whether that's explainer, appeaser, overfunctioner, or ghost—and doing something quieter, clearer, and more aligned. Here's how you can practice it:

Step 1: Name your default

What do I usually do when this cycle starts?

Do you defend? Try to be the reasonable one? Keep responding long after you've said what needed saying? Naming your autopilot move helps you step outside of it so you don't get pulled into the loop.

Step 2: Flip it, and expand it

What's the opposite of my usual reaction?

What are two other ways I could respond?

If you usually explain, what if you simply said, "I have already answered that." If you usually get pulled in, what would it mean to exit the conversation? Add two more: "I'll revisit this in writing" or "I won't continue this discussion right now."

Step 3: Try each option in your body

Say each sentence silently. Imagine pressing send or speaking the words. Do you feel clearer? Calmer? Less entangled? The *body yes* is not about comfort. It's about integrity. It says, *This is the choice I can live with.*

Step 4: Choose the one that aligns

Then use that choice. Calmly. Clearly. Without apology. You don't need to explain your decision. You don't need to win the conversation. You only need to protect your nervous system and the version of you that does not want to keep playing the same role anymore.

Flipping the script in these moments means you stop trying to make things better for them and start making them clearer for yourself.

◯Think of a current or recurring interaction that drains you. What's the script they expect you to follow? What would it look like to break that pattern, not to escalate, but to exit with integrity?

When you are dealing with someone who makes everything more complicated, it's easy to believe the conflict itself is the problem, but *how you engage* is what shapes your experience and your nervous system.

There is no need to convince them or win. You only need to choose a response that keeps you anchored in who you are rather than who they expect, provoke, or pressure you to be.

Sometimes that means staying silent when you'd normally defend. Sometimes it means walking away with a quiet "no." Sometimes it means saying what you need with calm clarity, even if your voice shakes a little.

That's the Exhale–Explore–Engage Method in these moments: clarity without cruelty, boundaries without blame, connection without self-abandonment. Maybe most importantly, it means knowing that you are not crazy, weak, or mean for struggling with these relationships. You are human. You've been conditioned to believe that calm equals connection, that responsibility equals fixing, that kindness equals surrender, but not here. Not anymore.

⟲Ask yourself: Which part of you most wants to be seen when you are in conflict with a high-conflict personality? What would it feel like to protect that part not by fighting harder, but by disengaging with dignity?

The more you honor your limits, the more space you create for your life, your relationships, and peace that don't require you to shrink, perform, or defend. That's the power of the Exhale–Explore–Engage Method.

By now, you've likely realized: Some patterns don't end because you found the perfect words. Some people won't soften, no matter how well you self-regulate. You can pause, explore, and engage with deep clarity and still find yourself in dynamics that drain, distort, or destabilize you.

When this happens, it does not mean you've failed. It means it's time to ask a harder question: *Is this relationship meant to be healed, or is it meant to be released?*

Knowing the difference is one of the most powerful acts of self-trust you can make.

What you've learned in this chapter:
- *Conflict with high-conflict personalities often escalates. You can't fix them, but you can protect your clarity.*
- *Your empathy is not a leash. You are allowed to pause, contain, and exit.*
- *Flip the script here means refusing to assume the role they cast you in.*

- ***BIFF/Three Cs (Clear, Calm, Contained) are techniques that support your nervous system.***
- ***Even with high-conflict people, you can choose your dignity.***

Chapter 14: When to Walk Away

"You can miss people and still choose to move on." –Alex Elle

There comes a moment in certain relationships—after countless conflicts, endless second chances, or a silence that has stretched too thin—when the question shifts from *How do I fix this?* to a far harder one: *Should I still be here?*

Not every relationship can, or should, be salvaged. For many of us, especially those who were raised to believe love means endurance, loyalty means staying, no matter what. And when our worth depends on how much we can tolerate, leaving can feel like failure. So we stay. We overextend. We try again and again—until we're no longer trying to repair the relationship; we're just trying to survive it.

This is not only about romantic endings. It's also true for family members who keep hurting you, friends whose silence cuts deeper than any fight, co-parents who use the children as leverage, and work dynamics that erode your peace, one micromanaged conversation at a time.

Leaving does not have to mean slamming the door; sometimes an exit can be made gently, slowly, and with great clarity, making a choice to step back from something that no longer reflects your truth.

◯Ask yourself: Is there a relationship in your life where you've done the work, paused, reflected, shown up with presence, and you still feel like the pain outweighs the possibility of repair or growth?

This chapter won't tell you what to do—you are the only one who has the insight needed to make decisions about your life—but it *will* offer you a way to discern. Walking away is not about giving up. It's about choosing peace for yourself over proving a point. It's about honoring your growth, your energy, your boundaries, and your right to live from wholeness.

Exhale: The Urge to Stay, the Urge to Run

When you stand at the edge of such a monumental decision, a particular kind of nervous-system noise often shows up internally.

Maybe it's a friendship where you've done all the reaching, or a family relationship that leaves you feeling shattered no matter how gently you try to hold it. It might be a dynamic that keeps pulling you back into versions of yourself you thought you'd outgrown.

Your body signals the first signs that something feels off: It could be a subtle sense of dread before meetings, calls, and holidays. Your body is not overreacting. It's trying to speak to you.

♡*Ask yourself: What does my body already know about this relationship that my mind is still trying to explain away?*

This is the moment the old survival scripts kick in:

Maybe I'm being too sensitive.

They didn't mean it like that.

If I just try harder, things could be different this time.

Walking away means I failed or gave up.

These scripts can lead us to override what we feel. We hold on. We repair with forgiveness. We rationalize and reframe until we don't recognize ourselves anymore.

Here's what I want you to know: The impulse to leave does not always mean you are escaping something hard. Sometimes it means you are honoring something real.

Before you make a decision, before you speak, ghost, apologize, or finally say, "I'm done," breathe. Settle into what's true.

Feel the Shift (When You Are Considering Letting Go)

Letting go is not just a decision; it's a process that unfolds in the body before it makes its way into words. That process often begins with a shift: You notice the body signal in the tightness in your chest when you see a message from them pop up on your phone; a pang in your stomach after another half-hearted apology; or a sensation that tells you the moment is more loaded than it looks.

Here's how to stay with that shift long enough to hear what it's trying to tell you:

Step 1: Notice sensations in your body

Ask: *Where do I feel this? What's happening inside me right now?*
Maybe it's a heaviness in your chest, pressure behind your eyes, tension in your hands or shoulders. Name it gently. Let it exist without trying to resolve it.

Step 2: Come back to the present moment

Ask: *What can I connect to right now that reminds me I'm here?*
Try anchoring your awareness to the contact of your body on a chair, the ground beneath your feet, the texture of your clothing, or the rhythm of your breath.

Step 3: Breathe

Ask: *Can I slow down the breath without forcing calm?*
Inhale through the nose. Exhale longer through the mouth. Repeat two or three times. Let each breath create space between the tension and your next move.

Ask yourself: When you think about letting go, where does your body respond first? And what happens when you stay with that response without acting on it right away?

This is how the practice becomes embodied—not by doing it flawlessly, but by remembering that every moment is a chance to return to yourself.

Sometimes the clarity does not come as a thunderbolt. It comes as a slow exhale. A quiet moment where you realize this is not yours to carry anymore.

Explore: What's Keeping You Here?

Making the choice to leave is not only about walking away from a person; it's about releasing a version of yourself that believed you had to stay—one who thought love meant endless endurance, whose worth depended on perpetually trying, and who learned that disappointment was somehow safer than hope. Walking away is never just a logistical decision; it's an emotional reckoning.

⟡Ask yourself: What part of me feels responsible for keeping this connection alive? Who taught that part that it had to try so hard?

In Internal Family Systems, this is your Protector. It wants to keep you safe from loss, guilt, rejection, or loneliness. Sometimes, however, the Protector is preventing you from accessing a wound that needs to be healed. You might be staying because of legacy beliefs: *Good daughters don't walk away from family. Real friends don't abandon each other. If I were more healed, this wouldn't bother me.*

The voice telling me that the good girls never upset their families was the loudest voice in my head for years. I kept showing up for holidays that left me feeling hollow, all because the Good Girl part of me was terrified of the guilt. It took me a long time to realize that my duty to my well-being was just as sacred as any role I had inherited. These are not universal truths. They are inherited narratives—and the more we challenge them, the more space we create for an honest decision.

Practice: Find the Pattern (Before You Walk Away)

Sometimes it's not the relationship itself that's hard to leave, but the story you've internalized about what leaving means. Before you walk away, it's important to pause—not only to weigh the pros and cons, but to get honest with yourself about what's making you stay.

Step 1: Spot the part

What part of me is holding on?

Is it the part that wants to prove you tried everything? Or the one who believes staying makes you good, strong, or loyal? Is it the part that still hopes the person will finally become who they promised to be?

Step 2: Ask what it's protecting

What is this part afraid I'll feel if I let go?

Shame? Guilt? Regret? Loneliness? Even if the relationship no longer fits, some part of you may still believe that walking away will mean failure or could trigger old pain.

Step 3: Trace the pattern and return to Self

Where did I learn that walking away is wrong or that staying is the only way to prove I'm worthy?

Then offer that part of you a few gentle words of reassurance: *Thank you for trying to keep me safe. I see you. I'll take it from here.*

⟁Ask yourself: Which version of you is having the hardest time letting go? What story is that part holding? What would it take to lovingly step forward from your true self instead of your fear?

What's the Real Fear?

Often, we're more scared of what leaving might say *about us* than the actual departure.

That we're selfish.

That we're too much.

That we'll be alone forever.

That we made a mistake investing so much to begin with.

Staying in a pattern that hurts is not a sign of loyalty, and leaving one is not a failure. It's a moment of choice where you get to decide *who you want to be* moving forward.

⟁Ask yourself: Who am I trying to be by staying? Who would I get to be if I walked away with love for them, for the past, and myself?

Now let's look at what walking away can sound like and what it means to exit a relationship—romantic, familial, professional, or platonic—with clarity and care, rather than rage, or collapsing into old survival strategies.

Engage: Letting Go Without Losing Yourself

There's no need to destroy relationships, but neither is it necessary to stay in a situation that is failing.

I was reminded of this truth in a recent, stark encounter. Out of nowhere, someone I used to be close to sent a message filled with rage and personal attacks—cruel names and accusations flying at me in a wall of words. It was the kind of message that makes your heart jump and your hands shake from a profound sense of violation. It was not an attempt at reconnection or resolution. It was an outburst of pain aimed squarely at hurting me.

In that moment, I knew that engaging would only pour fuel on the fire. So I chose not to. I didn't respond. I simply held my boundary. Disagreements are human; conflict can even be healthy when two people are trying, however clumsily, to understand each other. That kind of conflict has room for repair. This, however, was not a two-way dialogue. This was someone dehumanizing and blaming me out of nowhere, without any care for the impact.

That's where I draw the line. I won't allow a person to have the privilege of that kind of access to me out of self-respect. Someone else's pain is not mine to carry, and I am allowed to protect my peace. In practice, that meant no lengthy rebuttal, no defending myself, just a choice to disengage. I quietly blocked the person's number and took a deep breath, reminding myself that setting this boundary was not "mean." It was necessary. Sometimes the most compassionate choice (for you and them) is to simply refuse to retaliate.

Let me be clear: *Conflict and abuse are not the same.* A conflict arises when both people, even when upset, are genuinely trying to be seen or heard, retaining at least a sliver of mutual respect. An attack, however, is something else entirely: It's one-sided, designed to hurt, and devoid of any openness to understanding or repair. In those cases, walking away is wisdom.

If you've paused and listened, if you've explored the story and the legacy that keeps you tethered, what's left is choice—and not just any choice; it's a choice that honors your peace.

That's what **Engage** means here: a conscious decision to stop doing what you've always done—to stop bending, fixing, chasing, waiting, or staying silent to maintain a connection that's no longer mutual or safe.

Flip the Script: Choosing Release

Flipping the script does not always mean staying in the conversation. Sometimes it means choosing to exit the dynamic altogether, precisely because staying would require you to betray yourself, and you're done with that now. Here's how the *flip the script* practice can guide you when it's time to let go:

Step 1: Name your default

What do I usually do when I feel this is not working?

Do you keep trying? Keep explaining? Stay quiet to avoid more pain? Do you spiral in hope while staying emotionally unanchored? Name that pattern. It's been protecting you, but it may no longer be serving you.

Step 2: Flip it and expand it

What would I do if I weren't trying to earn love or keep the peace?
What are the responses that would honor my truth?

If you usually try again → What would it feel like to take a breath and step back?

If you usually explain → What would it sound like to say nothing at all?

If you usually hope they'll change → What would it mean to stop waiting?

New moves might include:

"This relationship no longer reflects who I am. I'm stepping away with respect."

"I have said what I needed to say. I won't be engaging further."

"I'm not angry. I'm just clear about my boundaries."

Step 3: Try each one in your body

Sit with each phrase. Say it in your mind. Where do you feel tight? Where do you feel light? Where does your body exhale, even through the grief? Find your *body yes*.

Step 4: Choose the one that aligns

When you make a choice that honors your peace, there doesn't need to be any drama, and you don't need to explain yourself ten different ways. Flipping the script here is not about walking away to punish. It's about self-preservation. Not every ending has to be comfortable, but it does have to be honest.

⊘Ask yourself: Think of a relationship that has asked more than it has given. What's your usual script? What would flipping it in a way that would help you reclaim your peace look like?

Sometimes the Exhale–Explore–Engage Method supports repair. Sometimes it's reframing, and sometimes it's release.

Release does not have to lead to a big scene. Release might sound like: "This no longer feels reciprocal, and I don't want to keep trying to hold something that's slipping away." Or, "I have tried. And I'm proud of how I have tried, but I'm done."

Engagement here is not about the other person; it's about engagement with your truth and a decision to stop engaging in the behavioral pattern in the same way. To stop explaining your boundaries. To stop hoping your needs will be met by someone who has repeatedly shown you that they cannot—or will not—show up differently.

Case Study: The Quiet Divorce

A client, Anna, had spent years navigating a friendship that had become increasingly passive-aggressive and emotionally draining. Every attempt at an honest conversation was met with defensiveness or deflection.

Anna kept thinking, *If I just phrase it better*, but after a final failed attempt at repair, she paused. She stopped trying to be heard.

And she wrote one last message: *I love who we were to each other, and I'll always be grateful for that, but I need something different now. I wish you well, and I'm stepping away.*

It didn't feel good, but it felt *right*.

Sometimes that's all you need.

Tool: Three Signs It's Time to Let Go

Use this reflection when you are unsure whether a relationship can be salvaged, or if it's costing you too much.

🗩 ***Ask yourself: Have I tried to repair this from a grounded place more than once? Has the dynamic repeated despite my clarity or boundaries? Do I consistently leave interactions feeling smaller or drained?***

If you answer yes to all three, you may not need another strategy; it might be time for an exit plan.

Affirmation: *I'm allowed to choose peace over patterns. I am allowed to leave, and I will still be worthy of love.*

This exercise helps you anchor your decision in clarity and groundedness. It also enables you to remember what's been true over time.

What If You Can't Say Goodbye Out Loud?

Not all exits are mutual. Not all partings come with closure. Some people drift. Some lash out. Some ghost or spiral.

In those cases, the difficult truth is that you may never get to say what you need to say. But that does not mean you can't let go. Letting go can be sacred and powerful, even when it's silent.

🗩 **Try this:** Write the message you'd send if you didn't need a response. Say what's true, what you've learned, and what you are releasing. Then decide whether to send it or simply keep it as your moment of release.

◯Ask yourself: What relationship in your life is asking to be released, where caring no longer has to mean sacrificing your truth?

Sometimes the most loving thing you can do for both of you is to walk away. There is no easy way to leave a relationship you once poured yourself into. Even when you know it's the right choice and your body exhales at the thought of distance, there is still grief. There might be second-guessing. There may be a part of you that is still waiting for something to change.

By all means, let that part speak, listen to its fears, but don't let it decide for you.

When we choose to walk away, it's because we finally recognize when a relationship asks more than it gives, when presence costs you your peace, and when staying would require you to shrink just a little more than you already have.

Letting go is not a failure—it's an act of self-love.

Love for the person you were.

Love for the person you tried to be.

Love for the person you are becoming, who no longer has to stay in old patterns that harm or wait in rooms where the door only opens one way.

⟳ *Ask yourself: What is one part of your life you are ready to release? What would it feel like to let go from a place of clarity rather than fear?*

We've talked about conflict—where it comes from, how it overwhelms us, and how it repeats. We've looked at what happens inside us and between us. We've named the legacies that shape our reactions, the roles we inherit, the stories we believe, and the hurt we carry. We've practiced breathing, noticing, and choosing. You've learned to pause, to get curious, to engage from a place of honesty that is deeper than fear.

The Exhale–Explore–Engage Method is not just a framework for conflict; it's a profound way of living. Let's explore what life looks like when you stop living from reaction and start leading from truth.

What you've learned in this chapter:
- *The Exhale–Explore–Engage Method includes choosing to release—not out of rage but out of truth.*
- *You can name your pattern, try new exits, and listen for the "body yes".*
- *Letting go can feel like grief—but also bring relief.*
- *Flip the script means breaking the loop with compassion.*
- *Closure does not need to come from the other person; it can come from self-alignment.*

Chapter 15: Living the Exhale–Explore–Engage Method

If you've made it this far, let's pause here—because that, in itself, is something worth honoring. You've walked through conflict in all its forms: the kind that flares inside your head, the kind that pulls you back into family roles you never asked for, and the kind that stings in relationships, drains you at work, and erupts in patterns that seem impossible to change. Through all of it, you've been actively engaged in the process of becoming *repatterned*, transforming not only your responses but the very way you experience conflict.

As a key part of your journey, you've practiced something most people never stop to do:

You paused.

You listened.

You stayed.

Even when your impulse told you to flee, to fight, to fold, or to fix, you slowed down just enough to notice that something else might be possible. You may not have gotten it right every time. That's not the point. The point is that you started making space between the trigger and the response. You started recognizing that your first impulse may not reflect your truth, and your legacy patterns aren't the only way to belong.

Maybe you haven't spoken your truth yet, have only set one boundary, or have just taken your first deep breath before hitting send on an email. That still counts. That *especially* counts because you are doing something most people spend a lifetime avoiding: You are learning to be with conflict without abandoning yourself.

⟁Think back to a moment, either recent or in the past, when you responded from presence instead of panic. What did that feel like in your body? What made that moment possible?

To live the Exhale–Explore–Engage Method means to keep returning to yourself when it matters most: to keep choosing, imperfectly and courageously, something more aligned than what you've always done. The more you do, the more your life will begin to reflect that choice.

From Framework to Practice

The Exhale–Explore–Engage Method began as a map: a way to intentionally navigate conflict rather than getting swept up in legacy scripts. The more you use it, the less it feels like a tool you have to remember, and the more it becomes the new default for the way you move through your life: quietly, naturally, one breath, one pause, one choice at a time.

At first, you'll apply it in the big moments: that difficult conversation with your partner, the family gathering that always presses your buttons, the tense meeting with your manager. You'll feel the impulse. You'll catch yourself mid-pattern. You'll pause, wonder, and shift course. It may feel awkward, slow, or even unnatural at first.

That's when you'll remember to *flip the script* as a way of being. Soon, you'll notice that you are already doing it without thinking. Your communication will become clearer. You'll pause before defaulting to an apology. When you hear someone's tone shift, you'll take a breath instead of immediately reacting. Emails will be sent without the extra paragraph of explanation, and instead of making a rushed decision to keep the peace, you will find yourself saying, "I need to think about that."

The Exhale–Explore–Engage Method becomes a nervous system imprint, a relationship pattern reset, a values-aligned way of living that you employ not only during conflict, but *before* the conflict even happens.

Micro-Practices That Become Habits

Here are some small ways you can start weaving the framework into your day-to-day life:

- o **Exhale: Feel the Shift.** Whether it's a tough conversation or a group chat message that triggers you, pause. Take three breaths. Wait until your body feels a little more grounded before responding.
- o **Explore: Find the Pattern.** Ask yourself silently, *What's the story I'm telling myself about this moment? What part of me is responding here?* You don't need to fix it. You only need to notice.
- o **Engage: Flip the Script.** Before speaking, emailing, posting, or texting, ask, *Does this reflect who I want to be in this relationship?* If not, pause and adjust. Consider the opposite response, and think of two more. Then move forward with the one that feels the most authentic for you.

Employing this method is not about scoring yourself. It's about seeing that even in the smallest moments, you are practicing something sacred: staying with yourself while navigating a relationship.

⌒*Reflection Prompt: What's one situation you used to dread or fumble through, but now you are able to meet with more presence—even if only slightly? What's changed since you started practicing the Exhale–Explore–Engage Method?*

What Becomes Possible When You Exhale, Explore, and Engage
When you stop living from impulse or habit, everything shifts: You stop feeling constantly behind in your own life, replaying conversations and wondering what you should have said.

You'll cease shrinking to stay safe or exploding in defense. Instead, you simply start noticing. In time, peaking with greater clarity will become second nature, allowing you to hold your boundaries without apologizing. You'll pause before making yourself smaller.

You may begin to find it easier to say, "I need a minute," instead of being swept away by reactive emotions, and you'll be listening more deeply—not only to others, but to yourself.

The other day, I burned dinner. The old me would have spiraled into self-criticism about being a *bad mom*. But the *repatterned* me paused, saw my son's disappointed face, and said, "Well, that's a bummer. I'm disappointed too. Pizza tonight?" There was no drama, no shame—just a shared moment of imperfection. That, I realized, is what peace feels like.

The ripple effect of this presence is profound: You'll feel it in how your relationships transform, in how your nervous system softens, and in how your mornings begin to feel less like tensing against life's ups and downs and more like living.

The Exhale–Explore–Engage Method promises something better than peace in every conversation. It promises *alignment*. Even when things get messy, you can trust yourself to respond in a way you won't regret later. You can stay connected to your values, even when others don't. You'll have the quiet confidence of knowing that your truth does not require performance or perfection to be valid.

One client told me, "For the first time in years, I had a disagreement with my mom, and I didn't collapse into guilt. I was able to hold compassion for her *and* not abandon myself."

Another said, "I stopped chasing after a friend who kept pulling away, and you know what? I finally felt at peace because I stopped trying to prove I was worthy."

A woman I worked with during her divorce said, "The biggest gift was not saving the relationship; it was saving myself from becoming someone bitter. I learned to pause, to feel, to say what was true instead of what was polite."

💬 **Try this:** Think back to a moment in your life, maybe years ago, when conflict overwhelmed you. What would it have been like to have this framework then? Now think about a moment coming up this week where you might need it. What would practicing the Exhale–Explore–Engage Method make possible for you?

Keep Returning Again and Again

Remember—this isn't about perfection. You won't always catch the moment in time, and that's okay. There will be days when you still raise your voice or shut down.

You might send the too-long message, say the thing you didn't mean, or stay too quiet when you wish you'd spoken. This isn't failure—it's being human.

The Exhale–Explore–Engage Method doesn't have a finish line. It's a lifelong practice, and like all meaningful practices, you aren't expected to do it flawlessly. All that matters is noticing when you've wandered off the path and gently choosing to return.

Again and again.

Each time you pause instead of snapping back, you are building trust with yourself.

Each time you name what's happening inside you, you are repatterning your nervous system for something different instead of reacting blindly.

Each time you choose a response that reflects your truth—not only your conditioning—you reinforce a new way of being.

It's natural to worry you are behind when you fall back into an old pattern, but you can gently remind yourself that you are in the process of learning to move from automatic to intentional, from urgency to alignment, from trying to prove something to presence.

◯ **Try this**: Next time you catch yourself mid-pattern, mid-apology, mid-overexplaining, or mid-withdrawal, see if you can take one breath and whisper inwardly: *I can choose again.* That's all it takes. That one moment of awareness is the turning point, and it is *always* available.

Tool: Integration Circle
In your journal, create three columns:

What I Used to Do	What I'm Practicing Now	What This Makes Possible
React immediately	Pause and breathe	Respond with intention
Overexplain	Speak simply and clearly	Feel more empowered
Avoid conflict	Stay in hard moments	Build a deeper connection

Invitation: The Exhale–Explore–Engage Method isn't a one-time achievement; it is practicing presence over time. Update this list monthly to track your repatterning progress.

When You Do Everything Right and It Still Goes Wrong

I need to tell you something I wish someone had told me earlier: Sometimes you'll exhale beautifully, explore with genuine curiosity, engage from your deepest truth... and *it will still fall apart.*

You'll choose your words carefully, speak from your values, stay regulated and present, and the other person will misunderstand you anyway. Or they'll hear you perfectly and still choose to leave. Or the conversation will end in a stalemate that doesn't feel like a resolution at all.

This isn't a failure of the method. **This is the truth of conflict.**

I had a conversation with my father a few years ago that I'd been preparing for months. I'd done the inner work. I'd traced my patterns. I knew what I needed to say and why it mattered. I exhaled.

I explored the fear underneath my hesitation. I engaged with love and clarity, speaking my truth without blame.

He didn't hear it the way I hoped. He got defensive. He brought up old grievances. The conversation didn't end in the tearful reconciliation I'd secretly imagined. It ended with both of us feeling misunderstood.

I drove home feeling like I'd failed. Had I not exhaled deeply enough? Explored thoroughly enough? Engaged skillfully enough?

Here's what is important: The Exhale–Explore–Engage Method isn't about controlling outcomes. **It's about choosing your integrity.** It's about being able to look back on a difficult moment and know that you showed up as the person you're trying to become, regardless of how the other person responded.

That conversation with my father didn't give me the closure I wanted. But it gave me something else: the knowledge that I'd finally said what needed to be said. That I'd stopped abandoning myself in that relationship. The external outcome was disappointing. The internal outcome was freedom.

When you apply this method and things still don't go the way you hoped, here's what to remember:

You are not responsible for other people's reactions. You can speak your truth with perfect clarity and compassion, and someone can still mishear it through their own filters, wounds, and patterns. Their response belongs to them.

Not every conflict has a resolution. Some tensions are structural. Some disagreements are fundamental. Some relationships can't hold the weight of honesty. The goal isn't always to fix the situation.

Sometimes the goal is to see it clearly enough to decide what you can live with.

Feeling disappointed doesn't mean you failed. You're allowed to grieve the outcome you wanted while still honoring the choice you made. These two things can exist together.

The method is about the long game. One conversation rarely transforms a dynamic. But each time you practice staying present instead of reacting, you're building a new neural pathway. You're teaching your nervous system that you can handle hard things and proving to yourself that you won't abandon your truth just because it's uncomfortable.

Sometimes you'll do everything right and still feel like you lost. Sit with that. Let it be uncomfortable. And then notice: *Did you lose, or did you simply not get what you wanted?* There's a difference.

Your integrity isn't measured by whether other people validate it, but whether you can stand in it, even when no one's clapping.

You Are Not Late, You Are Right on Time

If you've made it here, you've already done the bravest thing: facing yourself. You've learned that conflict doesn't start with the other person. It begins within ourselves—in our nervous system, in our patterns, and in our inherited stories. But now you also know that it doesn't have to end there.

You've practiced staying in discomfort long enough to hear the truth beneath your impulse. You've chosen to ignore the alarm. You've seen what it feels like to act from a place of clarity instead of collapsing back into old patterns.

That's what the Exhale–Explore–Engage Method is. It's the pause. The breath. The shift from *what I have always done* to *what feels aligned now.*

It's your ability to stay grounded in any situation, no matter the relationship, no matter the tension, and stay with yourself. To know that you are allowed to respond without explaining, to set boundaries without guilt, to ask for what you need without apology.

When you forget, fall back into old patterns, or lose your voice mid-sentence, you can still return. That's the magic. You don't need a new plan. You don't need to be "fully healed" to be present. You just need to remember: *Your power is in the pause.*

⟡Ask yourself: What's one area of your life where you are ready to try this practice?

The Exhale–Explore–Engage Method is not a magical escape from conflict; it's the profound discovery of the unwavering strength and wisdom already within you, enabling you to navigate any challenge with grace and authenticity. The path is now yours to walk—one conscious breath, one courageous choice at a time— back to your most authentic Self.

You are not late.

You are right on time.

Bonus Materials

Exercises for Practicing the Exhale–Explore–Engage Method in Daily Life

The Exhale–Explore–Engage Method at a Glance

Method	Purpose	Core Practice	Guiding Question
Exhale	Interrupt the automatic response	Feel the shift	What's happening in my body right now?
Explore	Get curious about what's underneath	Find the pattern	Where is my reaction coming from?
Engage	Choose a response aligned with your truth	Flip the script	What choice reflects my truth, not just my history?

Practices for Pausing

Here are a few real-world tools I use myself and offer to clients who are trying to practice this when it counts—in the heat of the moment:

1. The Physical Interrupt

Your body often moves faster than your thoughts. So, give it a physical cue.

- o   Press your feet into the floor and feel their contact with the ground.
- o   Gently touch your thumb to your forefinger, a simple movement to signal *pause*.
- o   If seated, shift your posture just slightly to interrupt the automatic stance.

These small acts re-anchor your awareness to the present moment. You are not "doing nothing." You are *actively pausing*.

2. The Breath-Bridge

This is more than "just take a breath." Try one of these methods:

- o   Inhale for four counts, hold for four, exhale for six. (This activates your parasympathetic nervous system, your body's built-in calm button.)
- o   Visualize the breath creating space around the feeling of urgency. Imagine it widening the gap between the trigger and the response.
- o   If you are with someone, take a drink of water. It buys you some time and signals thoughtfulness.

3. The Pocket Mantra

Words can help to create structure in the midst of an emotional flood. Find a line or variation that works for you and practice saying it under your breath or in your mind. Here are some favorites:

- *I can slow this down.*
- *There is no emergency.*
- *I get to choose how I show up.*

You don't need to believe it fully yet. You just need to plant the seed.

4. The Invisible Countdown

Before speaking or acting, count silently to three. Not to stall, but to listen to what your body is doing and to consider what the moment requires. Sometimes, by the time you get to three, your urge has already softened. Sometimes it might not, but you are in a different relationship with it now—one with more awareness.

5. The Permission Slip

One of the biggest reasons people struggle to pause is that they don't believe they are allowed to. That it'll make them look weak, disconnected, or like they don't care. So here's your permission slip: *It's okay not to respond immediately.* You are allowed to say, "Let me think about that for a second," or "Can we slow down?" Or you can pause without explaining it at all.

6. Track the Alarm

Bring to mind a recent reactive moment. Close your eyes and ask:

What did I feel in my body first?

What was I afraid of in that moment?

What memory does this feeling remind me of?

Say to yourself: *This feeling makes sense. I'm listening.*

7. The Two-Second Check-In (Pause. Pinpoint. Pivot.)

When you feel your body start to react in conflict, whether it's shutting down, flaring up, or preparing to flee, try a simple two-second practice to interrupt the automatic response.

Pause: Take one breath. Let stillness open before your next move.

Pinpoint: Name what's happening in your body: *My chest is tight. I want to disappear. I feel pressure to fix this.*

Pivot: Choose one small thing to do differently: stay present, breathe again, and try saying "give me a second."

8. Recognize the Rapids

Use this practice to recognize what emotional flooding feels like in your body and begin to separate sensation from story.

Instructions:

- o   Recall a recent moment when you felt overwhelmed by emotion in conflict.

o Without judgment, consider: *What did it feel like in your body? What thoughts showed up first? How did your behavior shift?*

o Complete the sentence: *In that moment, it felt like I was* __________.

o Reflect: *What part of you took over? What was it trying to protect?*

Practices for Exploring

Here are a few tools you can use to explore what's underneath the urge in the heat of the moment:

1. The Body Compass

This exercise, created by Martha Beck's somatic work, specifically the Body Compass process described in her book *Finding Your Own North Star*, helps you distinguish between a full-*body yes* and a quiet internal *no*. Your body has its own language developed through lived experience, even if your mind has not always learned to hear it. Here are the instructions:

Recall a *Yes* experience. Think of a time in your life when you felt deeply aligned, calm, confident, and true to yourself. It does not need to be dramatic. Just a moment when you felt like this was right.

Scan your body. Close your eyes. Ask: *Where in my body do I feel that "yes"?* What's the texture? The temperature? Is it warm, open, steady, and energized?

Recall a *No* experience. Now think of a time when you said yes to something that felt wrong, or stayed silent when something needed to be said. What did your body feel like then?

Compare the two. Notice the contrast. One might feel expansive. The other, constricted. One breathes. The other holds. When you're unsure what to say or do, imagine each choice and ask: *Which one feels more like "yes"?*

○***Practice using your body's cues this week. Try it on low-stakes decisions first. When a moment of conflict arises, remember: Your clarity may not come from your thoughts, but rather from your breath, your spine, or the space behind your ribs.***

Why the Body Compass Works

Your body is faster and wiser than your conscious mind. Long before you can explain what's happening, your nervous system has already made meaning through a process called neuroception. It constantly scans for safety, congruence, and alignment through sensation, rather than logic. When something feels aligned, your body opens. When it feels wrong, your body contracts.

The body does not always know what is "right," in a rational or logical sense, but it knows what is *true*. It remembers what you needed, what you gave up, and what you longed to say in the past. And it knows when a choice reflects your integrity.

Listening to your body also interrupts your *default mode network* (see Chapter 3) and reengages your somatosensory pathways, allowing for new neural associations to form. Simply put, *when you feel the truth in your body, your brain can follow.*

2. The *Is This True?* Pause

Borrowed from Byron Katie's *The Work*, these are deceptively simple but powerful questions:

- o   *Is this thought true?*
- o   *Can I absolutely know that it's true?*
- o   *How do I react, what happens, when I believe this thought?*
- o   *Who would I be without it?*

Try this in a moment when the urge is strong, whether it's to fix something immediately, shut down, or lash out. Instead of acting on it, pause. Ask what thought is driving the urge. Then walk it through these questions. Don't force an answer. Just notice what shifts.

3. Feel It, Then Frame It

Instead of jumping straight into analyzing or fixing, start by noticing any sensation.

⊘Ask yourself: Where in my body is this showing up? If it had a color, a shape, a temperature, what would it be? If it could speak, what would it say?

Once you've located it in your body, try framing the story it's holding. A few prompts:

- o   *This reminds me of the time…*
- o   *The fear underneath this is…*
- o   *The belief hiding here is…*
- o   *The part of me that's scared right now is…*

Don't worry about getting it "right." You are not looking for facts, you are listening for what wants to be heard.

4. The Rule Behind the Reaction

Every strong emotional reaction is trying to enforce a rule you've internalized. Here are some examples:

- o   *I have to explain myself, or people will leave.*
- o   *If I don't stay calm, I'm the problem.*
- o   *I can't let anyone see that I'm upset.*
- o   *If I speak up, I'll be punished or ignored.*

♡ ***Ask yourself: What rule is my body trying to obey right now? Where did I learn it? Do I still want it to be true?***

Sometimes simply realizing the rule came from someone else—or a younger version of yourself—can loosen its hold.

5. Two-Minute Inquiry

You don't need an hour. You only need *a breath and a bit of curiosity*. Here's a quick exercise you can use in the moment:

- o   Set a timer for two minutes.
- o   Close your eyes and place a hand on your chest or belly.

- o   Ask yourself: *What is this really about?*
- o   Keep breathing and *wait for the answer to land in your body,* not your mind.

You might not get perfect insight, but more often than not, something small and true will rise. A word, a memory, a sentence like *I'm scared of being blamed* or *I just want to feel seen* will come to the surface. Let that be enough for now.

6. Name It to Tame It

As neuroscientist and author Dan Siegel says, when we name what's happening, we reengage the part of the brain that helps regulate and reflect. Don't just say, *I'm upset.* Try to be more specific:

- o   *I feel dismissed.*
- o   *I feel unseen.*
- o   *I feel afraid of getting it wrong.*
- o   *I feel like I'm disappearing.*

The more accurately you name it, the less power it holds.

Crisis & Safety Resources

If you or someone you know is in immediate danger or a life-threatening situation, call 911 immediately.

Immediate Danger & Law Enforcement

911 – Emergency Services

The universal emergency number in the U.S. and Canada for police, fire, and medical emergencies when immediate assistance is required.

Domestic Violence & Abuse Hotlines

These hotlines offer free, confidential support, crisis intervention, information, and referral services 24/7.

National Domestic Violence Hotline

Call: 1-800-799-SAFE (7233)

TTY: 1-800-787-3224

Text: START to 88788

Chat: TheHotline.org

StrongHearts Native Helpline

A confidential, 24/7 culturally appropriate domestic violence and dating violence helpline for Native Americans and Alaska Natives. Call/Text: 1-844-762-8483

Sexual Assault & Dating Abuse Resources

National Sexual Assault Hotline (RAINN)

Call: 1-800-656-HOPE (4673)

National Teen Dating Abuse Helpline (Love is Respect)

Call: 1-866-331-9474

Text: LOVEIS to 22522

Mental Health & Crisis Support

Suicide & Crisis Lifeline

Call or Text: 988

Human Trafficking Support

National Human Trafficking Hotline

Call: 1-888-373-7888

References

Andrews-Hanna, J. R., et al. (2010). Functional-anatomic fractionation of the brain's default network. *Neuron, 65*(4), 550 – 562.

Barrett, L. F. (2017). *How emotions are made: The secret life of the brain*. Houghton Mifflin Harcourt

Beck, M. (2003). *The joy diet: 10 daily practices for a happier life*. Crown.

Beck, M. (2011). *Finding your way in a wild new world: Reclaim your true nature to create the life you want*. Free Press.

Bowlby, J. (1988). *A secure base: Parent-child attachment and healthy human development*. Basic Books.

Brown, B. (2012). *Daring greatly: How the courage to be vulnerable transforms the way we live, love, parent, and lead*. Gotham Books.

Dana, D. (2018). *The polyvagal theory in therapy: Engaging the rhythm of regulation*. W. W. Norton & Company.

Doidge, N. (2007). *The brain that changes itself: Stories of personal triumph from the frontiers of brain science*. Penguin Books.

Eddy, B. (2018). *5 types of people who can ruin your life: Identifying and dealing with narcissists, sociopaths, and other high-conflict personalities*. TarcherPerigee.

Frankl, V. E. (2006). *Man's search for meaning* (4th ed.). Beacon Press. (Original work published 1946)

Friston, K. (2010). The free-energy principle: a unified brain theory? *Nature Reviews Neuroscience, 11*, 127 – 138.

Goleman, D. (1995). *Emotional intelligence: Why it can matter more than IQ.* Bantam Books.

Gottman, J. M., & Silver, N. (2015). *The seven principles for making marriage work: A practical guide from the country's foremost relationship expert.* Harmony Books.

Hebb, D. O. (1949). *The organization of behavior: A neuropsychological theory.* Wiley.

Hochschild, A. R. (1983). *The managed heart: Commercialization of human feeling.* University of California Press.

Katie, B. (2002). *Loving What Is: Four Questions That Can Change Your Life.* Harmony Books.

Levine, P. A. (1997). *Waking the tiger: Healing trauma.* North Atlantic Books.

Lieberman, M. D., et al. (2007). Putting feelings into words: Affect labeling disrupts amygdala activity in response to affective stimuli. *Psychological Science, 18*(5), 421 – 428.

Linehan, M. M. (1993). *Cognitive-behavioral treatment of borderline personality disorder.* Guilford Press.

Maté, G. (2019). *When the body says no: Exploring the stress-disease connection.* Vintage Canada.

Neff, K. (2011). *Self-compassion: The proven power of being kind to yourself.* William Morrow.

Ogden, P., Minton, K., & Pain, C. (2006). *Trauma and the body: A sensorimotor approach to psychotherapy.* W. W. Norton & Company.

Perry, B. D., et al. (1995). Childhood trauma, the neurobiology of adaptation, and "use-dependent" development of the brain. *Infant Mental Health Journal*, 16(4), 271 – 291.

Porges, S. W. (2011). *The polyvagal theory: Neurophysiological foundations of emotions, attachment, communication, and self-regulation.* W. W. Norton & Company.

Raichle, M. E. (2015). The brain's default mode network. *Annual Review of Neuroscience, 38,* 433 – 447.

Rankin, L. (2019). *Mind over medicine: Scientific proof that you can heal yourself* (Updated ed.). Hay House.

Schore, A. N. (2003). *Affect dysregulation and disorders of the Self.* W. W. Norton & Company.

Schwartz, R. C. (2001a). *Internal Family Systems therapy.* Guilford Press.

Schwartz, R. C. (2001b). *Introduction to the Internal Family Systems model.* Trailheads Publications.

Siegel, D. J. (1999). *The developing mind: How relationships and the brain interact to shape who we are.* New York: Guilford Press.

Siegel, D. J. (2010). *Mindsight: The new science of personal transformation.* Bantam Books.

Taylor, G. J. (2000). Recent developments in alexithymia theory and research. *Canadian Journal of Psychiatry, 45*(2), 134 – 142.

Van der Kolk, B. (2014). *The body keeps the score: Brain, mind, and body in the healing of trauma.* Viking.

About the Author

Masha Rusanov is a conflict resolution expert, coach, and creator of the Exhale–Explore–Engage® method. Drawing on Internal Family Systems, somatic psychology, and conflict theory, she helps people break free from legacy patterns to live with integrity. Masha lives in California with her husband and their blended constellation of children. To learn more, visit www.masharusanov.com.